Single and STANDING

TORN CURTAIN PUBLISHING
Wellington, New Zealand
www.torncurtainpublishing.com

ISBN Softcover 978-0-6459696-1-0

Cover illustration by Meghann Weinstein. Used with permission.

Typeset in Meta Pro, Meta Serif Pro, Berlin Sans, Orpheus Pro and Connoisseurs.

Cataloging in Publishing Data
 Title: Single and Standing: Learn to Be Single, Date, and Thrive as You Wait
 Author: Brianna Rossi
 Subjects: Christian Living; Family & Relationships; Dating; Marriage; Life Stages; Love & romance; Love & marriage; Personal Growth; Singleness

Single and
STANDING

Learn to be
single, date, and *Thrive*
as you wait

Brianna Rossi

Contents

1

As Single as a Mushroom in the Desert

I STILL REMEMBER THE day I sat with my friends Sarah and Kelli on a three-way phone call booking our flights to Hawaii. We were so excited—ten days of ocean, sunshine, and every tropical paradise thing we could think of! The trip was still months away, but of course, even before the flights were official I had started planning. I was researching all the activities we could do when we got there, typing them into the inspiration document that Kelli had created for our trip. Definitely the *luau* with the traditional pig roast . . . hula dancing . . . kayaking to an island . . . eating coconut cake while being serenaded by Hawaiian music . . . a four-wheeling tour through the mountains where Jurassic Park was filmed. There were so many things we just *had* to see! And what was I going to wear?! I definitely wanted a floppy hat, a variety of bathing suits, and probably some sun dresses that were short because the weather would be hot!

From there, the story could have gone two ways. The first would be that I made it effortlessly to Hawaii and enjoyed absolutely everything that I had planned for, hoped for, and imagined. The other would be that when the day for traveling finally came, I would find myself in the wrong part of the airport, only twenty-five minutes before my flight was due to depart.

So there I was, standing in the middle of the terminal, scanning the list of flights, and realizing that my flight was not listed. I pulled out my ticket to look again at where my plane was leaving from: Terminal A. But I was not in Terminal A! Despite taking a fancy shuttle through the airport, I had somehow wound up in the wrong terminal. I felt my heart drop to my stomach. How does that even happen?! It might have helped if I had flown more than once in my life. Maybe then I would have known how to navigate an airport! Not only was I not at the right gate, I wasn't even in the right building!

I hadn't started to run yet, but already I was sweating and breathing heavily. I spun around to go back in the direction I just came from so I could hop back on the shuttle. Of course, the shuttle took forever to arrive! I was already pressed for time because of how stinking long it had taken to check in my suitcase. My stomach dropped down another level when I looked at the clock. It was one of those moments when there is nowhere to run but the adrenaline has already taken over. Everything in me thought moving would make the shuttle come faster, so I looked back and forth, wrung my hands, shifted my carry-on from one shoulder to the other, looked back and forth again . . . probably only thirty seconds had passed, but it felt like forever. When would the next shuttle come?! *This is an airport—you would think they could move things along faster than this!* I looked at the time on my phone, then tried to calculate how I could still make it to my gate.

I may have been in cool, calm and collected Hawaii-mode earlier that morning, but by the time I finally got to the right terminal, my mood had changed entirely. I looked around me through the crowds of people, trying to sort out where the signs were that told me where to go next but at the same time looking at them all too quickly to really register what I was reading. Having only navigated an airport once before, even locating the departure gate made me feel like a foreigner in another land. Add to that the adrenaline, and I'm pretty sure all the wheels in my brain stopped spinning so that my body could use the energy to panic. My mind kept going back and forth. *You're not going to make it . . . where is my flight listed? . . . oh, my gosh, I have to hurry up, I* **can't** *find it!* I tried to read the messages coming in on my watch and could feel my phone buzzing in my pocket.

"On the plane . . ."

"Where are you?!"

"They're almost done boarding! . . . Bri?"

I couldn't respond. I didn't have time! I kind of wanted to cry but I didn't have time for that either. *Ughh!* I grabbed my cheeks and pulled down like somehow stretching my face was going to transport me onto the plane. Then I started running—lopsided running, with my heavy bag weighing down on my right side. I was sweating, maybe crying, who remembers? All I knew was where I wanted to be . . . where I *needed* to be. But I was not there. My friends were on the plane, headed for our dream spot. I was not. I was late. I was left behind.

So did I make it?! Or did my friends go to Hawaii and experience all I had dreamed of, while I was left in an overcrowded airport terminal crying my eyes out? I'm not gonna tell you. Because right there in the uncertainty, with the unknown ending and the overwhelming feelings, is where it feels the story is often stuck when you're single.

~

Just like my trip to Hawaii gone wrong, sometimes we grow up thinking we are headed towards marriage only to find ourselves stuck in a place we never wanted to be, wondering if we will ever make it to where we want to go.

Maybe this is you—stuck in the metaphorical airport of life watching everyone else take off on planes to *your* dream destination. You can't figure out what you're doing wrong. You don't know why you're the one missing out. And you don't know what to do. Marriage is where you want to be, the place you have dreamed about. You have planned for this part of life, and if you're like me, you have done all the planning *way* in advance, like maybe even the before-you-hit-puberty kind of advance. You've pictured a loving man, a romantic engagement, a beautiful wedding with the most breathtaking dress. You've thought about color schemes, bridesmaids, honeymoon destinations, and the day you found out you would have a baby! But you're not there, maybe not even close. You just keep hearing updates about your friends who are moving forward: "On the plane!" or in other words, "Engaged!", "The wedding date is set!", "Pregnant!"

Your friends are boarding the plane destined for the wonderful world of wife and mom. Their destiny seems certain. But yours does not. You are late. You feel lost.

～

Okay, fine, I'll tell you. My longed-for trip to Hawaii wasn't actually that chaotic, but my journey to married life certainly has been. I used to think I would be married by twenty-four. It seemed like the perfect age since that's when my mom got married. But *give or take*, right? Twenty-five . . . twenty-six . . . twenty-seven. I remember the day when I had just turned twenty-eight and one of my best friends called to tell me she was engaged. She was also twenty-eight and, like me, had been waiting *so* long. We were FaceTiming as usual—only now she was sitting on the floor of her bedroom in the beautiful house where she and her fiancé lived, talking about shopping for her dress, the color her bridesmaids would wear, the life she was building with her soon-to-be husband. I was so excited for her.

When that call ended, I opened up Instagram and saw a post from my other bestie. It was her birthday, and her caption read, "This is twenty-eight!" In the picture, she was standing in the nursery of her house, holding her sweet, newborn daughter in her arms, wearing her husband's t-shirt . . . and in the background I could see their little puppy playing on the furniture. That was a beautiful twenty-eight! And for my newly-engaged friend, twenty-eight was filled with every dreamy detail too. But I was also twenty-eight, only I was still sitting on my mom's couch watching reruns of an outdated TV show. No husband. No baby. No beautiful home for me and my family. No puppy. No ring. No fiancé. No boyfriend. In fact, no guy even remotely on the scene. Nothing. I was as single as a mushroom in the desert.

It was a strange feeling because on one hand, I was filled with so much excitement for my friends. I wanted to experience all the joys of life with them. This meant I would go wedding dress shopping with my newly engaged friend, we would plan the bridal shower together and dream up ideas for her big day. It would be so much fun. We had been waiting forever for her boyfriend to propose . . . and he finally had!

I was excited for my other friend too. She had wanted a baby for so long. That right there was an answer to our prayers. There was so much celebrating to do, and I was sure her baby would be like my own little niece. But in addition to all the excitement I had looking outward, there was also pain when I looked inward. Would I ever experience all I hoped for too? And if so, *when*?! I didn't want my friends to miss out on a single thing they had planned for . . . I just wanted to reach the exciting destination *with* them! But how on earth could I catch up—or get there at all, for that matter? And how on earth would I survive this label of "Single" when so many people around me, including my baby sister, seemed to have discarded it long ago? They were living in the land that I dreamed about. I wanted to be there with them, but it was as if the plane to my marriage fantasy had taken off with all of them in it, and I was the lost, crying girl in the airport of singleness.

I know that I am not the only one who has felt lost and overwhelmed in the land of singleness. There have been times I have felt scared. I have wondered if the dreaming I had done for all these years would ever amount to the real, tangible experience of marriage that I desire so strongly. Dating has felt like that scene in Cinderella where the king's men try the glass slipper on the feet of about a million girls only to find that none will match the fit.

I have become incredibly discouraged when faced with a sea of no-fits. I have experienced the pain that comes with breaking off a relationship. It's the kind of pain that not only comes from sadness to see a relationship end, but also the fear and dread of having to start over again—having to wade through that murky sea of *no* after *no*, again and again. I have spent years at a time being solidly single. I have been a resigned single, a crying single, a single who felt she would die if faced with another day completely absent of physical touch. I've watched from a front-row seat as the people around me lived their lives. I have felt the longing in it all.

This book is not written to tell you how hard singleness can be. You know that already. You've been in the battle. I have too, but I have come to realize that the battle does not need to knock me off my feet. It's like the ten rounds of boxing—you may get the wind knocked out of you and fall to the ground, but you only lose if you stay down. Yes, I have been there, done that when it comes to the struggles of singleness, but there is so much more that I have experienced during this time. My hope is to share the things that have helped me. I want to share the golden nuggets, perspectives, and thoughts that have made a huge impact in my life but have lived as scribbles in my journal until now. I want to share all of it with you, and like a tour guide who has wandered around long enough to find the best trails, I want to help you navigate this crazy, challenging, confusing, breathtaking, enlightening and unique world of singleness—and best of all, come out standing!

2

Should It Be
This Hard?

ANYONE WHO WATCHED ME play as a child would have no doubt what I wanted to be when I grew up—a wife and mom. My aunt had gifted me my own white wedding dress when I was about six, with a handmade white bouquet, veil and all. I would play 'dolls' with my sisters, and each of us had imaginary husbands. All of these husbands came complete with first and last names and even awesome jobs (I mean, working at McDonalds is awesome, right?).

Whenever people asked me what I wanted to be when I grew up, my response was always the same, "A mom." You can imagine my disappointment when they informed me it didn't work like that—no one goes straight from childhood into being a homeowning wife and mother. There is another phase of life. A phase where you go from 'playing wedding' to dreaming about a real wedding. A phase where you watch romantic comedies and pin pictures of wedding dresses on your 'My Future Wedding' board. The other 'fun fact' I wasn't aware of, is that this so-called 'in between' phase could be really long, like *sometimes you wonder if it is ever going to end because it is taking so long,* kind of long.

If you are anything like me and have spent most of your life planning for the wedding-and-wife stage, then you have likely felt all the feelings that come with finally being at the 'right' stage of life (aka adulthood), only to find it looks completely different than what you imagined. The reality of your singleness doesn't match the vision you tenderly curated over all the years. At times it feels like the beautiful blueprint you designed for your life from when you were a child just got crumpled up and thrown in the trash and you have no idea where to go from here. This isn't as simple as waiting for the sequel to your favorite movie, or wanting something you don't have, like a new car or a fancy house. It's your life. It's *marriage*. It's family, children, life partner . . . all just hanging out in the deepest parts of your heart without any tangible evidence they exist.

I remember seeing a video on Instagram of a young woman like me who was desiring a relationship so badly. She was sitting in her bedroom, crying (all the dramatic body language was included). But it was the caption that caught my attention: "Single people who don't trust God." The message was that this single girl (who was clearly a mess) was an example of how people feel when they're *just not trusting God enough*. In theory, all she needed to do was trust that God had a plan, and all these sad feelings would go away. This aggravated me because it was a message I had heard so many times throughout my singleness—the message that, "If you were just spiritual enough, you wouldn't be struggling with singleness." If you were a 'good Christian', you would be content being single. You would simply know God had a plan, and that would be sufficient.

Now let me start off with a little disclaimer. Sometimes I've found it difficult to trust God in my singleness. Often, my struggles were the result of forgetting how powerful God is, or how much he loves me. However, there were many other times that my struggles had nothing to do with my faith. I was simply trying to process so many emotions. These emotions could not be wiped away by "just trusting God more."

Maybe you've had some of these feelings too. It's when you hear someone a decade older than you comment that she is *still* single, and you feel your body immediately react. Sure, she's talking about herself, but you're thinking about *you*, and you have to quickly rattle out the "Lord, please don't let that be me" prayer, just to stay grounded. It's that feeling that creeps in when you are around other people who are already married or in relationships. You may not be able to put a label on that deep-down feeling, but it kind of feels the same as it would to show up to a gala event and realize you're the only one wearing jeans. No one is actually *saying* you're inferior, but the feelings inside of you are saying it for sure.

And on that note, what about the galas? Okay, maybe you aren't going to many of those, but how about the occasional wedding, or party, or night out? You know the feeling of walking in alone—especially when you don't know many people there—and you have to make a choice. It's either walk in alone, or don't go. Do you ever get sick of those two options? I mean, how great would it feel to finally add a plus one to that RSVP card? Or what about the lack of physical affection? Does that get to anyone else? Because let's admit it, in this time of singleness we are seriously lacking in couch cuddles, or kisses, or the feeling of arms being wrapped around us. Our friends aren't jumping up to fill that void (thank God!) but that means every day that we are single is another day that physical touch is absent. Let's just say, the struggle is real, and can often be so incredibly painful.

And if that is not enough, what I have come to find is that there is often another feeling lurking around underneath all of that. It is the feeling that you should not be feeling these feelings. *Perhaps you're just doing it all wrong. Shouldn't you be handling this whole single thing better? I mean, you're a Christian, right?*

I'll admit that over the years, I have felt so much guilt in this area. I have struggled with all the feelings that come with being single, and at the same time I have tried telling myself that if I were a 'good Christian' I would not be feeling these things at all. If I were really trusting God, wouldn't I just feel completely content?

Or how about the idea that your struggle with singleness is not only wrong but might also be the reason you are single in the first place? Ever heard someone say, "You need to learn to be content being single before God will bring you a spouse?" Or maybe, "God won't give you a man (or woman) until you stop wanting one so badly?" I think the only belief worse than thinking you are doing something wrong by feeling pain, is the belief that your pain, or 'bad attitude' is what is keeping you from getting married.

I do not believe this sort of thinking reflects the character of God that we see in the Bible. God isn't withholding your spouse as some sort of prize for good behavior. He isn't playing mind games with you, or saying, "I know you want this, but first you have to stop wanting it, and then I will give you what you want." I mean . . . what kind of message is that? I will tell you what kind of messages these are. They are messages that misrepresent God's nature by claiming you have to act, do, or be a certain way in order for God to bless you. That isn't what relationship with God is like.

The Bible encourages us to make our requests known to God. Not, "Let's pretend we don't have desires, then once we've proven to God that we are holy enough, he will give us what we desire." That is not how God works. We have a God who wants to bless us and give us good things. We have a God who operates in grace, which means he not only gives gifts to his children, but he gives them even when they're not deserved. God created marriage, and he is not upset that you want to experience it. Your desire for marriage is a good one. God made marriage. And he is not put off by the fact that you want to experience that blessing. So continue asking God for it. The idea that if we truly found our joy in Christ we would never want anything else, takes away our humanity. We can love God with all our hearts and still desire his blessings.

～

Being sure about God's character takes the pressure off. The pressure that says you need to clean up your act and figure out how to be content, or else. The pressure that says you are holier—or handling things well—if you just *love singleness*. It is okay if you don't love being single!

While we're at it, let's reject the idea that if we were really spiritual, we wouldn't be struggling at all. This message has popped up so many times in life, and not only in my singleness. But I believe it's a false concept. Have you ever felt like you were in pain but concluded that this was a 'wrong' feeling? It's easy to think that if only our faith were strong enough, we wouldn't be suffering. It's an unfounded belief.

I remember when my mom was diagnosed with an aggressive form of breast cancer. The scenario is different from the one we are dealing with as singles. However, the advice she received was very much the same: "You need to just trust God." In fact, I remember a woman scolding my mom one day during a little 'breakdown moment'. This woman knew that my mom believed God had a plan for her life. Yet her comment to my mom as she was crying was, "You need to start walking the walk and not just talking the talk." In other words, if you trust God like you say you do, you should not be feeling all this pain you are feeling—you are handling this wrong.

The thing is, my mom *was* trusting that God had a plan. She knew that he saw her situation and that he was her 'very present help in times of trouble' (Psalm 46:1). At the same time, this didn't make it any easier to sit in a chemo chair or take away the dread of losing all her hair. My mom felt the scariness of the situation, the discomfort of the treatments, the unfamiliarity of suddenly being in sanitized medical territory, the starkness and sadness of it all, and simply not knowing if God's plan would ultimately match her plan. It was painful. It was hard. Should my mom have just taken it all in her stride, perhaps with a few somersaults along the way? Is this what we are supposed to be doing as Christians—minimizing our hardships and not feeling any complex emotions?

If we want to understand what trusting God in painful situations looks like, the best role model we can look to is Jesus. Think of the intensity of the physical and emotional pain he experienced when he went to the cross. In Matthew chapter twenty-six, we read the events leading up to that moment. Jesus was about to be betrayed, and as he was waiting for the hour the Roman soldiers would come to arrest him, he said to his disciples, "My soul is overwhelmed with sorrow to the point of death" (v. 38).

What intense feelings! Other gospel writers describe Jesus as being "sorrowful and troubled." He dreaded the cross, even praying that if it were possible, he would not have to go through this suffering. In Luke 22:41-44 we read:

> *"He withdrew about a stone's throw beyond them [his disciples], knelt down and prayed, "Father, if you are willing, take this cup from me; yet not my will but yours be done." An angel from heaven appeared to him and strengthened him. And being **in anguish [agony]** he prayed more earnestly, and his sweat was like drops of blood falling to the ground." (Emphasis and parentheses mine)*

Now, of course, I am not comparing what Jesus went through at the cross to our experience of being single. But we can see how Jesus, who is perfect, went through the experience of struggling—even though he had faith in his Father's plan.

The balance I see in this passage is that Jesus wanted the Father's will, and at the same time, felt painful emotions. He was trusting God, and at the same time, felt pain. He went to the Father for his strength, and at the same time, was in agony to the point where his sweat was as drops of blood. His trust in God's plan was there. But so was the pain. How insane would it have sounded if someone had told Jesus that the only way to express his trust in God was to face his situation without any tears?!

This is what I want you to know—you are not 'wrong' about how you feel. No, you are not going through the same situation as Jesus, but the message applies to any area of our life, including singleness. When you find yourself standing between what you long for and what is actually happening, it is normal to experience the whole array of thoughts and feelings that come with that. These emotions do not determine how godly you are. They don't determine whether or not you are deserving of a spouse.

I have learned, however, that our feelings do impact the quality of our life. As much as it is okay to feel all the emotions that come with singleness, we don't have to unpack and settle in with them. The sense of sorrow or frustration, or whatever it is we feel, does not need to become a lifestyle. Even in his pain, Jesus positioned himself to be strengthened (in his case, by angels). We too, can lean on God when it feels too much. Let's bring all our emotions to him. Not only can he handle them, he will help you handle them too.

I think of it like going to a physical therapist when your knee is hurt. Does the pain immediately disappear? No. But the physical therapist is there to help strengthen you. Without his or her support, you would likely fumble around a lot worse and for a lot longer. It is the same with God. We may not always experience immediate deliverance from our problems, but his insight, strength, and guidance are all essential in helping us on our journey. This season of being single may not be a dream, but it doesn't have to be a nightmare either. I want to share with you how I have come to rely on God for encouragement and momentum in this phase of my life, and how I have learned to trust—not in a cliché, "Just trust Jesus and everything is better" kind of way, but in a way that has really helped me to understand who he is. I also want to share with you the emotions I have faced, as well as how I have dealt with them.

The good news is that despair no longer defines my singleness. I still have rough moments, or even days. However, I have learned how to bring my mind and heart back to a place of peace, because ultimately, peace is where I want to spend most of my life. I still long to be married—there's no magic solution to get rid of that desire. I still hope marriage is coming soon. I still feel disappointed when milestones roll by and I had planned to be somewhere different. You know why I feel this way? Because I am human. As a fellow human, maybe you are experiencing fears, sadness, disappointment, frustration or pain in this season as well. I get it. However, as much as these feelings are completely normal, there is no need to sit with them for more than a brief visit. There is too much life to be lived right now, while you are alive, single or not!

3

When It's Happening for Them (and Not You)

MY LITTLE SISTER GOT married before me. And by "before me" I mean she had a boyfriend when I didn't, got engaged while I still wasn't, got married, went on a honeymoon, and bought a house and two puppies while I was still at the 'mushroom in the desert' stage. Wanna know what was probably the hardest part of all that? Watching it all when they were so cute and butterfly-like. When they were walking around holding hands, or cuddling constantly . . . in the same house I was living in. When they would lie all spooned up on the couch, and I was sitting on a wooden chair drinking my glass of water. When they were in their official relationship stage, and I was in my 'I'm gonna die if I don't get physical affection' stage.

I remember being upstairs and hearing the two of them saying goodbye down by the front door. Their little giggles, and lingering kisses . . . Oh. My. Gosh. I literally sat there and thought, *I can't take this, God!* It felt like a scene in a movie where they're torturing a prisoner by starving him to death while they sit there downing ice cream in front of him. No, I've never actually seen that played out in a movie, but that's how it felt. I was so close to the action, but in my personal life I was so far away that the closeness felt like torture. It made me want to jump out of my skin. Let's just say, if anyone wants to pass a 'no kissing in front of single people' law, I'd be there for it.

Even if you haven't watched a sibling being elegantly dipped backwards and kissed in front of you, you may have experienced the same feeling. I'm talking about the feeling you get when you see the engagement announcements on Facebook or hear a friend gush with excitement about all the romance that's happening in her relationship. It's the feeling you get at the movies or while watching a TV show, or in the constant stream of glistening achievements spread all over social media.

Whether we want to call it jealousy or a more agreeable word like *longing*, it is one of those human emotions we are all going to feel from time to time. It can be unbearable to want something so badly and still not have it, even when you've prayed for it long and hard.

It is not wrong or bad to feel these things, but I have found it helpful to realize there is a difference between an emotional response and a response *to* an emotion. An emotional response is not something you choose. It's the feeling that hits you when something happens. It's seeing someone's exciting, romantic story and sensing that tension rise in your chest.

What makes all the difference is how we choose to respond to these emotions. We can allow ourselves to overthink them until we are sick to our stomachs, or we can choose to focus on all the things we are thankful for. We can choose to draw away from our friends and be somewhat negative towards their exciting experiences, or we can fully embrace their celebrations. Either way, here's the good news—the choice is ours. I am not saying it's easy, but I will say it *can* be a game changer.

We are often unaware of the real impact of our responses until we are on the receiving end. I experienced this, when, for a brief period of time, I actually had someone new and exciting. For me, it was thrilling to be dating, because this was my first official relationship. Although it didn't last, for those few months I knew the excitement of finally experiencing something I had longed for.

So all my friends were happy and joined in the excitement with me—right? That's what I expected, but that's not what happened. Now, most of my friends *were* thrilled for me, but there were one or two who caught me off guard. These people had been very good at giving me advice in the past, but now there was a negative spin to their feedback. I would share something cute this guy had said, and their response would be, "He said that? I just think that's kind of a weird thing to say." Or someone would laugh as though his compliments were stupid rather than sweet and endearing. One girl randomly interrupted our conversation to interject, "It's okay to break up with him if you don't have feelings for him." That made me feel confused because I did have feelings. For a while this was hard for me to navigate.

I came to realize that those comments from a few of my friends were coming from their own hurt and disappointment rather than from their usual place of supportive friendship. They were single. They wanted boyfriends. If I was in their shoes—and I had been many times—I would have found it hard to listen to someone talk about something like this when I was longing for it myself.

This experience taught me that I don't want to show up in this way for my friends when they are the ones who are celebrating. I don't want to downplay their excitement so that I feel better. I have to stay aware of this because I can sometimes feel myself being pulled in this direction. For instance, if a friend is talking about how she wants to get engaged and I feel like telling her not to rush, I must ask myself if that's coming from a place of genuinely thinking she should slow down, or if it is my way of expressing that I personally want her to slow down because I don't like the way I am feeling about my own situation.

I'm thankful I have experienced being on the receiving end of these sorts of comments because now I can see both parts of the picture. When I am not the one celebrating, when their situation looks like my dream, I am not hearing *them* speak—I am only hearing my personal anxieties and fears echoing around in my mind. Downplaying someone else's celebration is not how I want to show up when my friends are experiencing something good or exciting.

The fact that I sometimes struggle with this does not make me a bad friend. It doesn't come from a place of wanting to hurt them. It comes from a place of my own pain. My emotions are responding to my experience. That isn't good or bad, it is just how I am feeling. In recognizing this I can give myself grace.

I have learned that, regardless of how *my emotions* respond, I can choose how *I will respond* to my emotions. This is the part that determines the way I show up for my friends. I remind myself that I love my friends. I want them to succeed. Yes, I may be struggling, but it really wouldn't change my situation if they were struggling too. Yes, I would feel less alone, but when I truly reflect, I realize I don't want the people I love to suffer too. I want them to flourish.

In reality, my short-lived relationship did not make them any more single. They were single if I was in a relationship. They were single if we broke up. Knowing this helps me when I look at my friends who seem to be getting everything that I long for. I try to separate my life from theirs and realize that what is happening for them is independent of what is happening for me. They are not making me more single or less married. They are living their lives. Whether I show up with a sullen attitude, or offer them support, the situation remains the same.

The only thing that changes is how I show up in my friends' moments of excitement.

But what do you do when you still feel the emotional jab? What do you do when you are watching your dreams unfold—only, it's not you they are unfolding for? When your story line is still wadded up in a ball in the back of a closet while someone else's is being played out in front of you, one social media announcement at a time? It's amazing how one diamond can make its wearer shout, "Yes!" while simultaneously making you internally scream, *Nooooo!*

What do you do? It starts with shifting your perspective. You remind yourself their story line has nothing to do with your story line. Something good happening for your friend does not mean it will not happen for you. What if we flipped our thinking to, *if God can do that for them, he can do it for me?* What if we took it as encouragement that the beautiful story we are hoping for exists? Yes, it might not be our turn right now, but that does not mean our turn will never come.

They say misery loves company, but why? If I am struggling right now, it doesn't actually help anyone if my friend is struggling too. Their excitement is not taking anything away from me. It is not holding me up or changing my story. We are two completely separate people. I am living my life and my story line, while they are living theirs. Yes, theirs may look better right now, but this is how life works—we all go through seasons. Each of us will have our own times of celebration. Right now, it may be their turn. Eventually it will be ours.

We don't all have exciting things—like buying a new house or car, meeting someone special, or having a baby—happening at the same time. While all this is happening, someone else may be suffering from an illness or may just have received extremely bad news. This is summed up very well in Ecclesiastes chapter three where it says:

"There is a time for everything, and a season for every activity under the heavens: a time to be born and a time to die, a time to plant and a time to uproot, a time to kill and a time to heal, a time to tear down and a time to build, a time to weep and a time to laugh, a time to mourn and a time to dance." (v. 1-4)

It is the seasons we are going through that make each of our lives truly unique. While one is mourning, another may be celebrating. This means you will have times when the focus is on your celebration and times when it is just not your season to shine. The truth is, your moments for celebrating life *will* come, even if right now the celebration belongs to someone else. No one can steal *your* story. No amount of good things happening for someone else will take away from the good things God has planned for *you*.

This helps us respond to those strong emotions. The reality is, choosing to respond positively to someone else's season of celebration stirs up other much more life-giving emotions inside of me. One of the most powerful choices we can make is to join in on the celebration. To look at that post, and instead of thinking, *Another one?! Why can't this be happening for me?*, you instead decide to switch your focus and think, *I'm glad it's happening for them*—especially when it's a person you love.

I have felt the power of this with so many of my close friends and family as they got engaged, celebrated a wedding, had babies, and bought houses. There was so much power in turning my focus outward, not inward. In doing this, I was able to say, "Wow, I love my sister, and I know how happy she must be right now. I am happy that she is happy" or, "My friend has been wanting a baby for so long. I am so glad she gets to experience the joy of having a baby."

Don't get me wrong, the emotions still rise up over and over again, but I have come to realize that if I am truly acting out of love for the people around me, their excitement becomes my excitement. I'm not talking about expressing fake excitement or pretending to be happy. Instead, I am pointing out that when you truly want the best for someone, you gain joy from seeing them experience it.

Sometimes it just takes a moment of deep reflection to find this joy. It may mean you consider how much you care about your friend and how you are glad they are not struggling right now. It may mean remembering to separate yourself from them enough to recognize that their excitement doesn't hurt you. Instead, the fact that you are a friend of theirs allows you to jump in on their excitement. Maybe you can take that leap and find ways to experience their excitement *with them* rather than wanting to yank them backwards into your situation.

It is important to emphasize that I am not suggesting you disregard your emotions. They are alerting you to the areas where you are most sensitive and tender right now, and you may need to take a little extra care of yourself. This could mean staying away from situations that heighten these emotions. Or this can be as simple as taking a break from social media if that is needed.

What I am saying is that both happy and sad emotions can be present at the same time. Focusing my attention outward on the people I love has helped me to truly be in touch with the part of me that is also happy for them. Happy emotions do exist within me and sometimes I just have to remind myself to turn my attention toward them. In doing so, I not only show up as genuinely supportive of my friends, but I also get to uncover my enthusiasm and bring it to the surface. That doesn't mean the hurt is no longer there, but it does mean it's paired with delight for my friends, and the more I have focused on that joy, the more I have found—in fact, that joy grows.

The happiness that comes from genuine excitement for others is a wonderful feeling. When I look back at my sister's wedding preparation experience, I remember it not only as a beautiful time for her, but also a beautiful time for me. I think of all the bonding I was able to do with my soon-to-be brother-in-law as I met him at the jewelry store to pick out the best diamond for my sister's ring. I think of the day I spent distracting my sister as he prepared to propose to her on the beach. I think of his proposal and get butterflies in my own stomach because of how much fun it was planning behind her back and discreetly convincing her to wear something pretty that day. I think of walking around beautiful venues and sampling foods for the wedding. I think of the bridal shower I got to throw where I decorated the cupcakes with seashells just like the ones on the beach where she was engaged.

All of it was so much fun, and I honestly believe a huge part of that was the result of me *choosing* it was going to be fun. I chose that I would enjoy all the fun little wedding things, even if they weren't for me. Being that she was my sister, and that my brother-in-law is a gem, I was able to be super-involved in her big day. That probably isn't always your level of involvement, and it isn't always mine either. In any situation it is as simple as deciding that if my friends get to celebrate then I am celebrating too. This is not to disregard existing painful emotions but to grab ahold of the joyful ones that are also there—often hidden underneath. I am inviting myself to life's party, whether I am the one sitting in the seat of honor or not.

This has meant I've shopped for the cutest baby clothes and accessories for other people's babies, I've bought cute little ring boxes as engagement gifts, I've handmade banners for bridal showers, I've bought sexy lingerie for brides to be, I've gotten thoroughly invested as my friends tried on wedding dresses and I have chatted with co-workers who are picking out everything from accessories, to flower colors, to top-notch photographers. I've done everything from creating a surprise bridal-party dance for my sister's wedding, to walking down the aisle in a tutu fulfilling a girl's fantasy of having ballerinas at her wedding. Trust me, the closer I can get to the action the more fun it is, but celebrating doesn't have to involve tutus and bachelorette parties. It can also be taking the time to pick out a card that says, "Congratulations to the new mommy and daddy," or sending a text that says, "Congratulations, you're a stinkin' fiancé!" when you hear the news.

Jumping in on the excitement helps you be an amazing friend—the kind of friend you are going to want when your celebration turn comes. It creates even more fun for the people in your life, and it's such a great way to love people and help make their moments special! As you choose to focus on the fun and the celebration that is going on around you, you will find that your own life will become more fun. Their blessings can bless you too—if you let them. Will you sometimes still feel those emotional jabs we talked about? Absolutely. And I know because they still come up for me. I also know that when they do come up, a decision has to be made. My mom always used to say, "Well you can be happy or sad, might as well choose happy." And honestly, that is exactly what I have learned to do. So when you hear about a friend's pregnancy and get that drop in your stomach, ask yourself how you can celebrate that little life entering the world. Buy the beautiful housewarming gift for a new homeowner and the cute puppy toys for the new puppy parents. Have fun with them in their fun season.

Romans 12:15 says, "Rejoice with those who rejoice; mourn with those who mourn." Put love into action like this, and before you know it, your season of celebration will be here. Don't wait until it's your turn, to celebrate the wonder of what's happening around you. Join in now, no matter who is on the receiving end. Let me tell you, this is without a doubt one of the best ways to show love to those around you, *and* it comes with a fringe benefit—it makes your life a heck of a lot more fun! Look around and see who you can celebrate with today. I guarantee there is someone waiting for you to jump in on their excitement.

4

But I'm Ready for the Next Part of Life

THERE'S A TREND I started to pick up on just by being with my friends. I have one friend who is in a relationship with her dream man. They look so cute together! She is a tall, stunning, blonde who fell in love with a dark, handsome man she happened to meet on a busy day at work. Sound like a romantic movie? It could be. He is super friendly. He is healthy and active. He is kind and generous. I mean, what more could my friend want in a boyfriend? So many girls would love to hear that scenario and be able to say, "That's me! That's my life!" Seeing the way they interact and watching them build their life is perfect. In my mind I can envision how amazing it would be if only I could be in that sort of situation too. It seems like this should be the next chapter of my life, and I want to be there.

I have watched my friend as she lives out *my* dream scenario. I want to be building a life with an amazing man like that. I listen to her as she talks. Is she talking about how amazing her life is, how blessed she is, and how so many of her fears about finding someone have been put at ease? Does she wake up with a sigh of relief each morning because she knows this amazing man exists and there he is, right there in her life? How amazing must that feeling be.

Believe it or not, that is not the main thing she talks about. Yes, from time to time she sighs and gives a little, "I just love that man." But most of the time she talks about something else—she wants to be engaged. She's thinking about the next chapter of her life, and she just wants to be there. Yes, sometimes she makes a comment about how great her man is, but I can tell by our conversations there are other thoughts that consume her.

She brings up out of the blue, "So when do you think he'll propose? How do you think he will propose? I want to move forward with my life, and this is the only thing I am waiting on! I need this to happen!" In other words, everything would be okay if she was just engaged. Then she could relax. Then she could enjoy her life. Then her life would begin moving forward. But not yet. She needs 'the next thing'.

Watching her, it seems almost crazy to me because I listen to her talk about how hard it is waiting to be engaged, and inside my head I'm saying, *Are you kidding me?! Do you even see how blessed you are? This man loves you. You have the assurance that the man you want exists! He has already told you he plans to marry you. You don't have to do the whole dating thing anymore or wonder if you'll turn old before the right guy walks into your life. You have him! You have an amazing relationship. So many girls would give anything to be in your shoes, and you are going to complain because the proposal part is a little slow?! You have all that, and yet you're going to obsess about not being engaged? Just chill and appreciate what you do have!*

But I can't say that. I can't even let myself think it. Do you know why? Because I do the same thing with my life. We all do it. We look at the next thing we want, and *the lack of it* becomes the main thing we see. Meanwhile, we miss everything that is right in front of us. How different would my friend's life be if she put aside the need to be engaged right now and spent more time enjoying these special moments while she builds a relationship with her man? She has something that is so precious. She could choose to savor it. I can observe this in my friend's life all I want, but it doesn't do me any good until I apply it to myself. There are so many times when I could really use someone saying, "Brianna, just relax and enjoy this moment. You'll very likely find a man, but right now, just appreciate what you do have."

Here's the truth: there will *always* be a 'next thing'. If you're waiting until you have a spouse to finally feel at ease, you are waiting for a feeling that doesn't exist. As humans we are always wanting the next thing. But the 'next thing' is just that—it's the *next* thing. What I mean is, getting what comes next on the wish list doesn't bring us completion. It doesn't satisfy all our desires or make us feel whole. Even when we get what we have been wanting so badly, we often move on quickly to the *next* 'next thing'. We spend so much time focusing on whatever we think will make our lives better. We obsess and daydream over what we long for, whether it's a relationship, a house, a degree, a business, a possession, or a career. We think that when we have that 'next thing' everything will finally feel okay. But it won't. It is not our circumstances that make us happy. If you are unhappy, unfulfilled and discontented now, you are going to be unhappy, unfulfilled and discontented when you are married. That is because contentment is a mindset, not something you can achieve by reaching your next goal.

What if we looked at what we have in front of us—at the dreams that have already come true? What prayers have already been answered? What do you and I have that other people wish they could have? Because honestly, I have been guilty of doing the same thing as my friend. The problem is not her lack of being engaged. The problem is not my lack of a relationship. The problem is that we are in the habit of focusing on our lack more than our abundance. We think about and even obsess over what we *don't* have. I have been guilty of being consumed with wanting a man. The thought pops up when I am driving in the car, when I am at work, when I am making dinner. Then I see my friend who doesn't have to think about finding 'the one' all day long, and I think, *that must be nice! She has the perfect solution to my overwhelming thoughts, fears, and desires—she has a man.* But she doesn't have an engagement. That is what plagues her mind when *she* is in the car, at work, and making dinner. The trend here seems to be, it doesn't matter what we have, we will naturally focus on our lack if we don't intentionally turn our focus onto our blessings.

I see this over and over in myself, and in the people around me. One friend couldn't wait to get pregnant. Then once she became pregnant *(yay!)*, she was fed up with the constant rib pain. She talked about how much she hated the experience of pregnancy and how much she wanted the 'next thing'. That baby needed to be born, *then* she would be much happier. Another friend planned her wedding *(yay!)*, but even before her wedding day she and her fiancé were focusing on how awful it would be to live in an apartment—they had to have a house to move into. So, they got married, and they bought a house *(yay!)*. Now they had both things! Everything should have been good, right? No. Now they needed a puppy. Their family just wasn't complete without a puppy. They got a puppy. Would you be surprised if I told you they can't stop talking about when they'll have a baby?!

All this sounds crazy when you are watching others—when it is other people who are constantly thinking about the next thing while they could be enjoying what's in front of them. But what if it's me—or you? *Is* it you? It has been me! I think it is something we all do. It's part of our human nature. For me, marriage seemed like the moment I would 'make it'! That's when I imagine this uncertainty I have felt will end. That's when the searching ends, and the dating, and the scanning for single men every time I walk into a new room. That's my 'when I get there' moment. It's when I finally get there after I have been waiting all these years. It's at that point, where I am no longer single, that I finally 'make it'.

Movies can make a wedding seem like getting married is the conclusion, and everything after that will be 'happily ever after'. Just because we are inclined to think like this does not mean we have to live like this. Ask yourself, "What am I giving the most attention to in my life?" Do you think more about what you want, or about what you already have? Focus on what you *do* have. What you want will one day become a reality, but until then, here's the truth—yesterday's wants might already be today's reality.

What do you have right now, that you once longed for? What is it that you already have that someone else may really want? Focus on that. It is great to have dreams for the future, but don't let your dreams cause you to miss what is right in front of you. There was once a time when you prayed for the things you have today. Appreciate those answered prayers.

If you recognize yourself as the person who thinks, "I am nowhere near where I thought I would be. I hate it, all across the board," then I have a challenge for you. What one thing have you always wanted to do that you can begin doing right now? How could you start taking steps in that direction? Even small victories are victories. In the meantime, choose to savor what you've got.

My sister always used to laugh at me when we went on family vacations because I would say several times while we were away, "Guys, savor this!" She laughed, because even though I was so passionate about my advice, I would say it at the most random times . . . while the whole family was sitting together in the car . . . while we were applying sunscreen in the parking lot at the beach . . . while we were drinking gas station slushies with our eyes all red from being in salt water for so long. They weren't the most incredible moments, but my point was pretty solid. We were on vacation. We were together. We needed to make sure we didn't just *go* on vacation, but that we really *experienced* it. I looked up the word 'savor' in the dictionary and most of the definitions had to do with food. But there was one definition that stood out to me: *to savor, to have the experience of.*

Are you treating the blessings in your life like checkmarks on your wish list, or are you truly experiencing them? Even if you have nothing else amazing right now, you have your youth. You will never be as young again as you are today. Are you experiencing it? You have your independence. Are you savoring it? This takes intentional effort. That is why the younger version of myself would shout out to my family, "Savor this!" It was because I knew we needed that reminder to help us enjoy whatever moment we were in. Even if our eyes were red and stinging, we were at the beach and we were together, and that was worthy of being appreciated.

This is something I have learned to do in my singleness too. I can focus on being single, because that is definitely a part of my life right now, or I can focus on other parts of life. In my family vacation scenario, we could focus on the fact that our eyes were a little irritated and our cheeks were a little sunburned, because those were real things. But it was important not to miss the fact that we were on the beach. We were in the sunshine. We were together as a family. We had been able to save up the money for that trip. We were building memories.

In our lives right now, we need to make sure we're not missing the amazing things around us because we're zoning in on our singleness. I am not saying that turning our focus onto the beautiful things we have will take away the desire for a spouse. It won't, and it shouldn't. There is nothing wrong with wanting to be married, and no amount of 'happy thinking' has ever made me stop wanting marriage. However, focusing all the time on what I lacked only left me feeling defeated and miserable. It is possible to maintain these desires yet move them to your peripheral vision instead of keeping them in the spotlight.

What do I mean by that?

I grew up as a ballet dancer, so dancing in the spotlight was a big deal! On a stage, the spotlight draws attention to the primary focus of the dance—the principal dancers, who captivate and engage the audience. Does this mean the audience cannot see the other dancers on the stage? No. However, these sideline dancers no longer make as much of an impact. Whoever is dancing in the spotlight leaves the biggest impression on those experiencing the show.

In our lives we can choose what we place in the spotlight. Is it shining on your unmet desires, highlighting all you are lacking? Does your mind constantly meditate on the fact that you are single, and that your life doesn't look the way you thought it would? If so, it's no wonder you feel discouraged and frustrated. The beauty of intentionality is looking at the things you are grateful for and pulling *them* into the spotlight. The Bible encourages us to practice this saying,

"Whatever is true, whatever is noble, whatever is right, whatever is pure, whatever is lovely, whatever is admirable—if anything is excellent or praiseworthy—think about such things."
Philippians 4:8

My singleness does not define my existence. Single is a relationship status, not a summary of your life. What else makes up who you are? What accomplishments are you proud of? I remember sitting at my sister's graduation from nursing school and my mom said, "I wish I had done something like that." Two years later, she did. At the age of fifty-four my mom went to nursing school and trained to become a nurse. Now she works as a nurse. It has become such a part of her routine that she could forget to appreciate this if she didn't stop and intentionally savor the experience of being a nurse.

Do you have something like that in your life? What do you take for granted? What did you once want so badly that you now have? If your response is, "Nothing," I would challenge you to look a little deeper. If you still don't find anything of note, then what can you create? What can you step into in life that you will be proud of in the future? Turn your focus to the things you could easily overlook.

There are lots of ways to be intentional about this. Many times, I have written out gratitude lists on paper or typed them up on my phone. For a while I kept an 'appreciation album' on the camera of my phone. I would take pictures of anything I thought was special throughout my week. I took a picture for my album of a plant my friend gave me so that I would take the time to appreciate that special friend. I took another picture of an invite my brother-in-law sent me to join him in an app-based daily Bible reading plan, because I wanted to take a second to appreciate the sort of relationship I have with my sister's husband that he would even send me something like that. I also wanted to intentionally appreciate that fact that he loves the Lord—especially since I had always prayed that my sister would have that in a husband. I took a picture of my other sister painting the bedroom wall with me, simply because I was having fun hanging out with her. I even took a picture of my workout session with my sisters. They weren't great photos or even outstanding memories. They were just little snapshots of my daily life: relationships, things I owned, moments that were special—anything that I normally wouldn't take the extra time to enjoy. Adding these pictures to the 'appreciation album' that I created on my phone was my way of saying, "Savor this!" and it helped draw my attention to all the simple, special parts of my life that are not often in the spotlight.

That was my little plan of action, but do whatever *you* have to do to pull yourself into the here and now. Find a creative way to bring attention to your blessings, and get thinking about your list.

I remember my friends and I had a game night on New Year's Eve. None of us had kids except for one friend, Emma, who tucked all three of her little munchkins into bed and then came to play with the rest of us, her single friends. We played a game called 'double ditto'. In this game someone reads a prompt from the game card, like, 'Hobbies for rich people'. Then everyone has to come up with two answers, like, 'Flying', 'Polo,' or 'Sailing' to write on their piece of paper. Then you figure out how many other players thought of the same answer as you—ditto! One of the prompts was, 'Things you prefer to do by yourself'. We all started thinking of things that are sometimes done with other people, but are better on your own, like studying or sleeping. When we asked what Emma's was, she laughed and said, "Peeing?" Of course, that wasn't a ditto, because literally not a single one of us had ever been in a situation where we thought, "Ughh, I wish I could just pee by myself!" It's clearly a taken-for-granted luxury! But to Emma, this was the first thing that came to mind.

That goes to show there are so many things we can enjoy right now that we don't even think to enjoy! Honestly, sometimes hanging out with my married friends who have children is the best reminder of this. Like when someone asks, "Want to go get ice cream?" and I immediately reply, "Sure!" while someone else has to say, "Let me check with my husband and make sure he's good with the kids awhile longer," or, "I really shouldn't. I need to get back for the kids' bath time." Those are things I never have to think about! So, get creative with *your* list. Write down the things you already have that are amazing, but also write the things you don't have to deal with in your singleness. No getting permission from a significant other over here! I don't have to share a bathroom. My money is all 'my' money! I don't have to deal with any crazy in-laws. I can watch what I want on TV and don't have to suffer with the golf channel. Whatever you can think of to bring your focus back to the things that you *do* have now! You may want to breathe a sigh of relief at the thought of this 'singleness season' ending, but just remember that when this season passes, it takes along with it a lot of the perks that are attached to it. You have those perks now! Make sure you don't take them for granted!

This act of intentionally turning your mind to the things you appreciate is not something you do once. You have to do it over and over. This has become my go-to way of refocusing. On extra rough days, take a moment to write your lists or to read out the lists you have already written. It may sound like a lot of work, but I guarantee it is not as exhausting as listening to your internal dialogue of sorrows and worries.

If you are thinking, "Yeah, yeah, yeah, I can write lists of what I appreciate, but that only lasts a little bit, then I am back to thinking again," you may be right, it may seem like something you have to do repeatedly. But think about how you got to the place you are now— where your lack of being in a relationship rules in your mind. Did you spend one day thinking how much you hate being single and then suddenly fall into a pit of despair that has lasted for months or years? No. Thinking about your lack has become a practice. You have thought about it from every angle. You have likely thought about it in the car, in the shower, cooking dinner, and lying in bed at night. Getting into this habit didn't happen overnight—it took time. Likewise, if you want to get used to savoring life's special moments, you will have to be willing to put as much practice into creating this new habit. Learn to dwell on all that is good, and watch it create genuine joy within you. This is helpful advice, whatever our stage of life.

Another piece of advice we've all probably heard is, "Don't compare yourself to others." I mean, we know that, right? We usually get told this when we are feeling lousy about our own life and the person next to us is doing something great, and we know comparison is pointless because we can't possibly have what they have. But what we sometimes fail to realize is that comparison is just plain deceitful.

Let me show you how comparison works. My friend Amber looks at her friend Danielle and thinks, "I wish my husband was as attentive as Danielle's. He's so sweet and nurturing. He even brings her flowers each week. I wish my man was thoughtful like that." Her own husband, Jeff, can't compare in that respect. He isn't great at giving compliments, and as for expressing his feelings, he isn't great at that either. When Amber looks at Danielle's husband, she can see all those traits that she wishes she had in *her* husband. But let's imagine she was actually married to Danielle's husband. Would she have everything she wanted? *Absolutely not!* Because here's the thing about Danielle's husband—he's just not Amber's type. In fact, he is the complete opposite of what she is attracted to. Not only that, she has nothing in common with him. Her own husband is very athletic like she is, and they have a great time going out to socialize. Danielle's husband would rather do his art and lounge around at home. In reality, Amber would never choose to be married to someone like Danielle's husband.

Amber doesn't see the whole picture of Danielle's husband. She stares at the bouquet of flowers and thinks, "I wish *I* had that!" What she is missing is the fact that Danielle's husband is a complete person. Yes, some of what she sees in him is exactly what is missing in her own life. At the same time, if she were to do a husband swap, she would have just as much missing—if not more.

Now I don't think Amber actually sits there and wishes she was married to Danielle's husband. But I do think she isolates his positive traits like add-ons when you're buying a car. It's as if she thinks, "Hey, I like this bundle, can I add it on to my current model?" Unfortunately, humans don't work that way. We aren't mix and match, we are entire packages. We all have areas in our lives that are thriving, and other parts that are lacking. Our successes, failures, family dynamics, personality struggles, habits, hobbies . . . each person's life is a whole package.

The next time you're tempted to look at one element of someone's life and think, "I wish I had that," remember that you are staring at only an isolated part of a whole life. As nice as it would be to add the positive elements of their life onto yours, it doesn't work that way. Just as you have aspects of your life that you love and things that aren't so great, that person does as well—they are just different from yours.

I am not trying to make you feel better by telling you to search for what is wrong with everyone else. I am just pointing out that we are so quick to look at one personality trait or one feature of someone's life and immediately feel our situation is inferior. Instead, we could look and realize, yes, they have that and I don't, but that doesn't mean I am missing out. It just means that my life looks different. In my own life, I can see the highs, lows, and everything in between.

As a final note—stop romanticizing. To romanticize is to see something as better or more appealing than it really is. Yes, marriage is beautiful, and being in a relationship is amazing. At the same time, we sometimes get so caught up envisioning the romantic moments . . . the white dress . . . walking down the aisle . . . waking up next to the love of our life . . . falling asleep to a goodnight kiss . . . building a home together and creating a beautiful family. We create this beautiful picture of our future as so ideal, and so desirable, that our current life situation of singleness can't compare. This is the damage that romanticizing does. It makes us entirely focused on the good points of another season, exaggerating those good points in our heads until our life right now seems so inadequate in comparison.

The truth is, the next season of life will have great parts and hard parts too. The key is to discover how to enjoy life right now because marriage, or whatever is the 'next thing', is not the magic ingredient that makes life fantastic. Making the choice to focus on the good parts of the season you are in—yes, even singleness—will make this season the best it can be.

Here's an activity you can do: write out a list of the things you appreciate about your life right now. Write down the things you take for granted. Write down anything you have that other people would love to have. Write down the advantages you have in your singleness right now that you may not have in your married future. Write down everything you are thankful for. Find ways to turn your attention to the little things in your daily life and choose to take a few moments to *savor* them. It is amazing how things change when our mindset shifts from seeing this as a *waiting season* to a season we can *savor,* even while we pray for what we want. Do this over and over again, any time you need a little pick-me-up.

5

Behind the Scenes

I WONDER WHAT GOD is doing in your life right now. What is he thinking? What is he working out on your behalf? What is he doing with all the prayers you have prayed? Most likely, you are saying, "I don't know! I have no idea. That is exactly why I am frustrated!"

Not knowing what God is doing is one of the best ways to summarize our problems. We have been standing in this same place. It seems like nothing is changing, and it hasn't for a while. We don't know what God is doing. You probably resonate with the frustration of that statement, but do you ever think about the hope it contains? Think about it. The fact that you have no idea what God is doing, does not mean he isn't doing anything—it just means you don't know what it is yet.

The emotional reaction in my life, tied to the thought that nothing is happening, makes me remember my friend Allison and how she felt a few years ago. She was in a relationship, but she and her boyfriend had fought again and again over the same thing. The latest fight had been the most heated.

"We're still not engaged!" Allison angrily yelled at Kyle. "I cannot believe you still haven't proposed to me! Are you *ever* going to marry me?!" It had been almost four years, and this had been Allison's most frequent complaint for the past two. She wanted to get married. She was with a great man, but nothing was changing. She was not any more engaged to him now than she was two years ago. He was still not officially committed to her. She still had no ring.

"Would you stop pressuring me?! Proposing is the man's job!" Kyle yelled back, frustrated that she was trying to take over what he saw as his job—the proposal.

She responded, "If it's your job, then why aren't you doing it? I'm done waiting!"

Allison sat there venting to me about this fight and I felt almost as mad as her. This was getting ridiculous. Kyle had said in the past that he knew she was the one for him and that he wanted to marry her, but that was some time ago. If he was serious about her, surely he would have done something by now—like propose. On top of that, it was now December, and they just had a conversation about their vacation plans for the upcoming year. She suggested dates she thought would be best for them to travel, hoping his response would give her an idea of what was going on in his head. Perhaps he could take time off in April? She was thinking he might use this vacation time to plan a trip for the two of them—maybe a romantic trip where he could propose! But his schedule at work was too busy to take any time off January through April. Then she suggested October or November. If he was secretly planning to propose he would probably want time off at the end of the year for their honeymoon. But he didn't want to take time off work then because that was when his seasonal sports started up again.

Now that she had a rough idea of Kyle's plans for his sports, vacation and family time sketched out in her mind, she put two and two together. He had no plans for marriage in the year ahead. No plan for a little proposal-getaway. No plan for a summer wedding. No plan to go anywhere for a honeymoon at any of the times she had suggested. He was just continuing with life as usual. The steps they were taking this coming year were the same as they had taken in the previous years. Not a single glimmer of change was in sight. Marriage was not even on his radar.

The week they'd had that serious argument was a bad one for Allison. That's when she started to realize the life she was hoping to have with Kyle was not going to happen. When we talked, she cried. She had spent so much time envisioning their future together. She had hopes and dreams. It was an incredibly low moment in her life as she tried to process what was happening. She had told Kyle at least a hundred times that she wanted to get married, but nothing had happened. At this point, her future was no longer filled with hope. Looking ahead there was only pain, fear, and emptiness.

Have you ever felt this way in your relationship with God? Like you have been praying for something for so long, asked so many times, and it's getting exhausting? Have you ever looked at your scenario and felt that you were running out of hope? Looking at the way life is going it seems pretty clear you will not be getting what you have been wanting any time soon. The emotions that come with reaching that conclusion are painful to navigate. And yet, things can change quickly.

I was astonished when later that week, Allison sent me a very unexpected text. A picture of her—with an engagement ring on her hand. *What the heck?! He proposed?* It came out of nowhere. Or at least it seemed that way. I called my friend immediately. My initial thought was that maybe Kyle had finally caved because of their fight a few days earlier. However, that was not it at all. The truth was that Kyle had been planning the occasion for months, and Allison had been completely taken by surprise.

While it appeared their life together had been slowly circling around in the same old, redundant pattern, Kyle had been thoughtfully planning out every detail of his proposal to create an absolutely perfect evening. While she was at work, he had taken time off, gone to the jewelers and worked with them to design a unique ring—one that matched the exact description of the ring Alli had raved about. When the jeweler presented him with a great ring, Kyle had sent it back and requested some fine tuning to make it even better. He didn't want to give her a *nice* ring, he wanted to give her a ring that far exceeded her expectations. He would check it, critique it, send it back. Apparently, he repeated the cycle multiple times over the span of several months, giving attention to every detail. He hadn't forgotten about the proposal for a moment. The only reason Allison felt so hopeless was that nothing seemed to be moving forward. Yet all of the details were being worked out behind the scenes where she couldn't see them.

Every day, Kyle was adding another piece into the puzzle to bring her dream into reality. A few weeks before he wanted to propose, he planned to visit Alli's parents. Again, while she was at work and without her knowing, he drove all the way out to her parents' house to ask their permission to marry her. He couldn't skip this step . . . she wouldn't have wanted him to! But each of these steps prolonged the time before he could go ahead and propose. This delay had spiked Alli's impatient, aggravated, outbursts. Even so, he waited out of love for her until the plan was fully prepared before he revealed it.

The proposal turned out to be perfect for my friend Allison. The time of year was perfect for her. The way he proposed was perfect for her. The style of the ring was perfect for her. The words he used to ask for her hand were perfect for her. She could not have designed a better proposal if she had done it herself.

Alli now looks back and admits that as much as she had wanted it to happen earlier in their relationship—several years earlier, in fact—she was glad it happened in the timeframe it did. She sees now how the delay caused her to develop as a person. By the time he asked her to marry him she was better suited for marriage. Their relationship was in a much more grounded place than it would have been if she had jumped into marriage back when she wanted to.

What does this now happily engaged woman's story have to do with us besides making us sit in our singleness drooling over another sweet, little romance? Well, their story helped me to see parallels in the story of my life. Like Alli, I go about the day-to-day process of waiting for my marriage in a very similar way. I cry a lot. Then there are times I feel okay. Then there are days I freak out because I 'know' that nothing is happening. It looks to me as if my life is just circling around in the same old way. Sometimes I'm fine with that. Other times, I have a breakdown moment and I think, *God, this is your job! Why aren't you doing it? I am done waiting!* I've spoken to God in that impatient, demanding way many times—just like Alli. And every time it feels justified, because just like Alli I have been asking for a husband for a long time—so long that it's starting to feel ridiculous. Peering into the future I have tried to see if I could spot the answer to my dreams on the horizon. I couldn't. I have made calculations, I have summarized all the points—it's just not going to happen. How have I come to such a definitive conclusion? By looking around I have seen clearly that nothing is happening. At least that's what I think I have seen. The truth is, I have no idea what is going on behind the scenes.

Alli's story helped me. I walked in it alongside her, and I wholeheartedly arrived at the same conclusions as her. Nothing was happening. Kyle was doing nothing. Her future was not going to turn out the way she wanted. And you know what? We were both completely wrong. This helped me to see how very little we actually know. What we are able to see with our own eyes is such a tiny fraction of the whole picture. For Kyle, the proposal was being planned—every day the moment was getting closer, but Alli lived out those days in worsening aggravation and anxiety because she was only able to see a small fraction of the full story. We had both accepted these 'truths' about her future while never acknowledging that there was an entire behind-the-scenes production taking place out of the range of our sight.

This is where the parallel between Alli's story, and my story as a single woman, really hit home. She was dealing with 'flesh and blood' yet was blind to so much of what was going on. I am dealing with a supernatural, miraculous God who operates beyond what I can physically see—or even comprehend. Yet my not being able to see God at work did not mean he was *not* at work in my life. Having no idea what the heck he was doing did not mean he was not doing anything. It simply meant I couldn't see it.

This thought, *I have no idea what he is doing now,* creates new and exciting possibilities. What *is* he doing? What *is* he planning? How *is* he pulling things together on my behalf? I don't know. What I do know is that I have a God who loves me and wants to give me my heart's desires. Do I think he would allow me to be single for longer than I want if that means giving me the very best gift he has for me? Yes. Do I think he feels sad when he sees me upset and crying? Yes. And might he *still* withhold his gift until the right time because of his love for me? Yes. Do I think he plans things with the same attention to detail that Kyle did? Yes, and honestly, I'm sure a lot more!

God's version of pulling all the pieces together is not as simple as running in and out of a jewelry store or privately visiting the in-laws. He operates behind the scenes at a level we can't even comprehend, working in the lives of those around us, guiding our steps and decisions so we end up in the right place at the right time, developing the character in us that needs to be developed. The amount of detail that will go into bringing our spouse to us is insane, if you think about it. But God cares about every single detail.

We need to remember this in our relationship with God. Often we ask him for what we want, then go about our lives concluding that God is not doing anything just because we can't see any progress. We have no idea what God is doing—just like Allison had no idea what Kyle was doing. But that does not mean nothing is happening. It simply means we can't see it yet.

If we know we have a God who oversees our life's production, why do we get so disappointed when we see only the empty stage? Does an empty stage mean no work is being done behind the scenes? As a dancer, I can tell you the artistic process is far more extensive than what the audience gets to see on the day of the show. I don't know about you, but I don't always remember that this place behind the scenes of our life exists. So much more is happening than our eyes or even our hyperactive imaginations can comprehend.

None of us is promised marriage—and I always hate it when people remind me of that—but I believe that marriage is a wonderful gift and a good heart's desire. I don't get a guarantee I will get married. However, I know that I have a God who loves to give me good gifts, whether that is marriage or something else that is beyond my imagination. Matthew 7:9-11 says,

> *"Which of you, if your son asks for bread, will give him a stone? Or if he asks for a fish will give him a snake? If you then, though you are evil, know how to give good gifts to your children, how much more will our Father in heaven give good gifts to those who ask him?"*

If our parents (and Allison's fiancé) can give good gifts, imagine how much more God, who loves you, can give you amazing gifts. Remember, when you can't see the whole picture—he can. No matter what his plan is, it will be good.

Let me summarize: *Seeing nothing happen does not mean nothing is happening.* Seeing no change does not mean there is no progress! There is more to the story than what you can see. You don't know everything—in fact, you probably know a lot less than you think you do. Things may be taking longer than expected, but it does not always mean they are not going to happen. God's work is often done behind the scenes, and when the finished product is revealed, it will blow your mind. It's time to speak truth to our fears. Alli's fear was not based on truth, but only on what she could see. The same applies to us. We may not be able to see what God is doing, but the truth is, he is working it out perfectly for you—the timing, the method, and the gift itself.

Late one night, I was in bed trying to fall asleep, but I couldn't. I was totally worked up thinking about the last guy I had seriously dated. Just to give you some perspective, it had been two years since I had dated this guy. When I ended the relationship I believed I was doing the right thing. I was devastated at the idea of having to start over, but I was convinced in my heart that it was the right decision for me. Fast forward two entire years of singleness, and here I was, lying in bed, wide awake, heart racing, thinking, *What if I did the wrong thing?* I had now been single for two entire years and still there were no prospects in sight. The dates I had been on since then were completely dull. There was nothing on the scene that resembled real potential.

That night, I just couldn't shake it—I was in full-blown freakout mode. *What if he had been the right guy? What if God had sent him to me? What if I'd had my chance and missed it? What if I had messed it up?* I was terrified by the possibility that maybe I had missed 'the one', that

I had let him go, and now, two years down the road, it was too late. *Had I made the biggest mistake of my life?* My midnight, panic-stricken brain couldn't handle the thought that the answer to my prayers may have been right there in my hands and I had given it away. I remember rolling over in bed and saying out loud (which you can do when you live alone), "God, *please* let me have done the right thing with him. Please let that decision have been right!" As a woman longing to fall in love and get married, I *needed* that decision to be right, because by now it was a done deal. I couldn't bear to think what my future might look like, or the consequences I would have to suffer if I had made a wrong decision.

Maybe you haven't experienced this same thing, but has the thought crossed your mind that you might not still be single if you had done something differently in your past? What if you had been more social, or less picky? Would things have been different? Maybe you grew up in conservative Christian culture and thought dating was wrong, and now you're wondering if all those years of not dating were detrimental. Maybe you have your own version of feeling like 'somehow I might have just messed it up' somewhere along the journey. It's not a good feeling, is it?

After that sleepless night, I got up, dressed, and went to work. Around ten o'clock that morning, I left work to run an errand. As I was driving, a text message popped up from my mom. It said,

> "Just a random thought. You 100% did the right thing about (insert ex-boyfriend's name)."

I was in shock. Where did that even come from?! I had never mentioned to my mom that I was struggling with these questions. Remember, I hadn't seen or even talked about this guy in over two years!

I called Mom right away and asked, "Why did you send that?" She replied, "I was just praying, and it came to my mind, so I told you." I could not believe it. God had given me the reassurance I had cried out for just the night before! As I drove back to work, I bawled my eyes out. I was so touched by the fact that even two years later, while I was in agony over my decision, God took the time to hear what I said and acknowledge me. He knew the details, he saw the whole picture, he cared about my worries, and he was telling me so clearly that I hadn't messed it up. *I didn't miss it. I had done the right thing.* This doesn't always happen, but it was a pretty cool experience. I felt like it was God's way of saying, "Even though you don't know what's going on, I do."

Now, I know you might be thinking, "I wish God would give me clear signs like that!" Honestly, I have said that myself in so many situations . . . *I wish God would just talk to me!* The thing is, sometimes we do get some clarity from God like this. But the whopping majority of the time, it's not quite so clear.

The takeaway I want to give you from this story is: God cares about even the little details of our lives. He cares about the relationships, the people we've had a crush on, the breakup emotions, the worries we have in bed at night, and all the tears we cry into our pillow. That moment was one of God's ways of reminding me, "I see you—I've got you." And that is not true just for me, but for you too, because it's true of his character. Whether you are hearing from him clearly or not, he sees every detail, he is involved, he does care, and you are not alone in this. God cares about small details, like our feelings and our fears, and he cares about the big ones like who we will marry.

6

The Freak-out
Moments

HAVE YOU EVER WATCHED *The Lord of the Rings?* I'm one of the rare people who hasn't, but I've seen enough to know that one of the characters is Gollum. He's a creepy little guy with stringy hair and crooked teeth who crawls around searching for 'the ring' while muttering under his breath, "You don't have any friends. Nobody likes you." Sometimes my thoughts sound like my own little version of Gollum in my head: "You're not as successful as your married friends." "You're gonna be single forever." "You aren't where you should be in life, I mean . . . look at *them*."

It doesn't take much for this mindset to take over. All I need is to hear my younger sister talk about having babies and immediately I get hit with anxiety. It's as if my creepy little companion peeks his head around the corner and says,

> "Ooh I heard that too . . . looks like she's going to be married *and* have babies before you."

> "You don't even have a boyfriend."

> "Is there even a man in sight?"

"The kind of man you are looking for probably doesn't even exist."

"Maybe you're just going to end up being the fun aunt."

Does anyone else have thoughts like these, or is it just me? *What are other people thinking about you? Are they wondering why you can't find a man? Maybe no one is interested in your life because you have nothing exciting going on. If only you were getting proposed to, or had spicy love stories, or wedding plans, or a pregnancy announcement. What do you have? Oh yeah, a close relationship with your mom? Loser.*

I've heard them all—all of the various versions of how my life looks nothing like it should. How it might end up disappointing me. How long I've been single. How my dating hasn't worked out in the past. How I don't have any possibilities in sight, and how, statistically, that's not likely to change. I collectively refer to all these overwhelming, anxiety-provoking trails of taunting thoughts as my 'freakout moments'.

Now by 'freakout' I'm not referring to having actual panic attacks, although this may be the case for some people. I am referring to those feelings of uneasiness, worry, anxiety or fear that rise up the more I let these thoughts roll around in my mind. Do those kinds of Gollum-like thoughts pop into your mind too? If so, do they create some unsettling emotions that make you feel a little like freaking out?

The tiniest things have sparked these feelings in me. Someone falling in love in a movie . . . sometimes not even falling in love, just kissing (and honestly, sometimes they don't even have to be kissing, they just have to be *talking* about kissing) . . . and the next thing I know, my mind has taken the seemingly foreign thought of physical affection down the freakout rabbit hole. It's me listening to my extended family talk only about my younger sister's future since, ya know, she's the only one who seems to be building a future at this point. It's having yet another birthday where I'm still single, or being alone on another

New Year's Eve. It's listening to a conversation about someone's 'normal' love life and feeling the anxiety rise up in your chest. You so badly want to change the conversation or run away from it, but either way it's in your head now. All your fears about being single forever, and all your insecurities about your love life, are like an overstuffed closet—someone pushed everything in and slammed the door. It only takes a little conversation, a milestone, or a social media post to slightly crack open the door, and *boom*—your emotions come tumbling back out into the forefront of your mind.

I'm quite the artist when it comes to imagining stories of my future inside my head. Unfortunately, the genre that I have often focused on when writing my life's imaginary narrative is often, ummm . . . let's call it *tragedy*. Some of my freakout moments start off relatively chill with a small discouraging thought like, "Wow, thirty and single. Never thought that one would come." And then next thing you know I am envisioning what I'll be like when I'm forty-five—loveless, childless, a cat-lady. *Disclaimer: I don't even like cats.*

Some freakout moments are mile-long thought-trains. I go over where I went wrong in the past, how I need to change what I'm doing in the present, and then I'm envisioning the worst-case scenario of my future. This is usually what keeps me pondering in the shower for forty minutes instead of washing my hair.

Have you ever had these moments? Maybe 'moments' is too small a word. Maybe I should say whole weeks that have been filled with painful thoughts. Whole days when you were stuck on one part of your singleness and couldn't shake it. What about the big, old slumps you had to keep functioning through? That's me too.

What is really going on when we're experiencing freakout? Are we just a bunch of lunatics who can't get a grip, our lives all scattered and out of control? Or are we just people who are dealing with a disorienting case of *expectation versus reality?* I say it's the second option.

The bottom line is, we aren't freaking out over nothing. We are freaking out over what sometimes feels like everything. All of society, forever, has told you where you *should* be right now. You know where you want to be. You're not. This wasn't the plan, and sometimes you feel like you're an off-the-rails train smacking into tree limbs and rolling through muddy grass. That's a tough place to be. If you find yourself there, don't let the freakout character run rampant. Remember, he's not always right.

My friend Sarah is a psychiatrist at a prestigious hospital in Philadelphia. The positive side of having a friend who is also a psychiatrist is that they tend to psychoanalyze you. The negative side is also that they tend to psychoanalyze you. I think the most annoying thing Sarah ever says to me is, "Sounds like you're catastrophizing." I hate when she says that because it translates in my mind as, "Stop being dramatic, you're just making stuff up." However, sometimes I take a step back and ask myself, *Is there some truth to that? Am I catastrophizing, or in other words, creating imaginary scenarios of the worst possible outcome? Have the things I am feeling upset about actually happened?*

Trust me, the scenarios in my mind all feel highly probable to me in the moment. If I had to, I could tell you all the details of my present situation which have made me want to jump on the freakout bandwagon. The fact that it's been a long time since I met any guys I find even remotely interesting makes me feel like I have no options and that I will stay this way forever. The fact that I am watching my sister and my friends celebrate anniversaries and move through milestones while my life stays the same makes me feel as though I will continually be stuck in this place. The fact that the dating apps haven't brought me anyone great yet makes me think I'll never have much success using them.

I could go on and on about all the reasons I think my friends will have kids in elementary school before I even pop out a baby. I can tell you all the reasons why I'm afraid of what I'm afraid of. All my logic and reasons make sense. This is why I get annoyed when Sarah calls me out on the legitimacy of my conclusions.

But although it's frustrating, it is helpful to stop and evaluate what is happening in my thought life. Am I focusing on the worst-case scenarios? Am I habitually meditating on the unfavorable future I could get stuck in?

One of the questions that is so hard for us to answer is: If life is not going to look like what I planned, what will it look like? This can be a scary thought, and our minds can come up with scary answers. But you know what? The majority of the things we have been anxious over probably haven't happened. Yes, you may know exactly why you think things will turn out one way, but in actuality perhaps they won't. We spend so much time worrying that our life will fall short of our expectations. But here is the truth: It may not. I like to think about this sometimes: *What if everything turns out okay and I spent today worrying for no reason? What if my future exceeds my expectations and I look back and think, I wish I had just relaxed back then—it all turned out fine?*

One night I was worrying that I would be that person who never ends up getting married. What if my worst fear came true? My hope was that God would give me what I asked for, but I was also pondering how I was going to handle it if that expectation was never met. That's a heavy thought to consider. But then I was reminded that the Bible describes God as able to do "immeasurably more than all we ask or imagine" (Ephesians 3:20).

That's when it hit me. I had been worrying that God would fall short of my expectations, or just hoping he would meet them. But what if I focused on his ability to *exceed* them? He is capable of doing more than we imagine. What if we become more attentive to his abilities, rather than living in fear? Again, there is no guarantee we will get everything we want in life, but there is also no guarantee that we won't. There is great peace to be found in choosing to hold onto the fact that we have a God on our side who wants to bless us and who is capable of doing immeasurably more than we can even begin to envision. What if it all turns out okay? What if all this time God has been working on a life for you that will exceed anything you have asked for?

Flipping the Mantra

I challenge you to try flipping around the narrative when you are tempted to think the 'what if' thoughts.

"What if I'm still single by the time I reach forty?"

Flip it around. "What if I'm married by then and I'm just wasting my time worrying about something that will turn out just fine?"

"What if the guy I marry isn't attractive?"

Flip it around. "What if he is more attractive than I ever envisioned?"

"What if everyone else has kids before me and I am left in the dust?"

Flip it around. "What if that means my baby comes at a super-special time? And even if it is later than everyone else's, what if that's fun? What if that means my baby is the latest and greatest excitement and gets to have some great role models?"

"What if there isn't anyone who is a right fit for me? What if I'm single forever?"

Flip it around. "What if I'm not single forever? What if I end up with absolutely everything I ever wanted in a husband, lifestyle, and kids?"

Have you thought about this? Even if marriage doesn't happen, is it possible your life could still exceed your expectations? Deciding to flip our mindset like this is what living a life of faith looks like. Hebrews 11:1 says, "Now faith is confidence in what we hope for and assurance about what we do not see." Faith is the ability to believe something exists when you cannot yet see it with your human eyes.

A lot of people scoff at the idea of faith saying, "I'm not going to act like something is real when it isn't yet." But here's my question: Aren't we already doing that with fear? When we walk around afraid of how our future will turn out, terrified of never getting married, assuming that our lives aren't going to live up to our dreams . . . and when we allow these thoughts to get us down and make us feel hopeless about the future . . . are we not acting like something is real, that isn't yet?

Your future is unknown to you—that's true. You cannot *yet* see it with your eyes. Yet you have the choice to believe that things will never get better, or that 'better' could be coming at any moment. You have a choice to believe that someone, or no one, is out there for you. You have the choice to keep pressing forward or not. If you are experiencing fear over what your future may look like, try repeating this: "I believe my life is going to be better than I imagined. I believe things are going to change. I am excited for what is happening next in my life." In other words, "There are many ways my future can look. I am going to choose to live today as though tomorrow and every day after, is only going to get better."

Learning to Chill Out

One morning as I was leaving for work—pushing it with time as usual—I got stuck behind an old-lady driver. I love old ladies, but when they are driving incredibly slowly in front of me, my love starts to shrivel up a little. I live at the back of an apartment complex. Exiting from the complex leads out into a cul-de-sac where you can turn left or right. Either way you go, you will meet up at the traffic lights that lead to the main road.

As I was driving out of my apartment complex, headed towards the cul-de-sac, I realized that the little old-lady driver in front of me was in no rush at all. She took her time adjusting her mirror to get a better view, then started gently rolling along while looking around and gazing out her window. I did not have time for that. The second we reached the cul-de-sac she gingerly . . . carefully . . . slowly . . . turned right so as to not hit a dip in the pavement. I whizzed out and quickly turned left. We would end up at the same traffic lights, but thank God, by that time I would be in front of her. When I reached the intersection leading onto the main road, the traffic light was red. I stopped and looked in my rearview mirror to see if she was coming. She was, but of course she was ridiculously far behind. *Thank goodness I didn't stay behind her!* I said to myself. *I would have never gotten to work on time!*

Some seconds passed as I waited for the light to turn green so I could turn left onto the main road. Eventually my little old-lady driver rolled up next to me, looked both ways a couple of times and . . . slowly turned right *on a red light* to continue on down the main road.

There I was, still stuck at the red light at 7:25 a.m. Exactly one minute later I turned left onto the main road thinking, *Oh my gosh. If I had stayed behind that lady she would still have turned right on the red, and I would still have been stuck there at 7:25. I might as well have relaxed and enjoyed my drive.*

I'd been proud of myself when I first arrived at the red light and saw my elderly neighbor lagging way behind. I'd thought, in all my frustration and angry driving, ranting and raving, that I'd beaten the clock and conquered time. But I hadn't. I had literally changed nothing. One minute later, at 7:26 a.m., I turned onto the main road. The only difference was *how* I had gotten there. I had huffed, got more and more anxious, drove a little wildly, and thought, *Good thing I'm not behind her. I don't have time for this!*

But what if I had just chilled out? What if, instead of getting all worked up, I had enjoyed my music and enjoyed the drive? When you think about it, if I had just enjoyed my morning drive, I would still have turned into the main road at 7:26. I would have arrived at that time if I had freaked out. I would have gotten there at that time if I had stayed calm.

I noticed my reaction and thought about it. *This is how we often live life.* We want to be married. We want to have kids. We want whatever the thing of the moment is. We know God is in control. But we spend the journey freaking out—anxious, aggravated, trying to speed things up. We miss the sunshine coming in the window, we miss the music playing on our radio, and instead we continue pushing forward in a frenzy.

What's the main message I took from this story about me and my neighbor—my little, old-lady driver? Freaking out doesn't necessarily change the destination, but it changes whether or not we enjoy the journey. In my singleness, freaking out was not causing me to find a husband any faster. It actually made me a grouch. It made me anxious. It made me spend a whole evening pacing my living room in tears. But it did not make me un-single.

Remembering Reality

Let's pretend for a second that you find your 'right person' in another five years from now. I know, I know, you definitely don't want to wait that long and I'm right there with you. For the sake of our sanity let's just say we know that's not going to happen. The thing is, we really don't know, so before we start freaking out over that idea, let's say this—it probably will not be that long. But for the sake of my point let's pretend you're going to be single for that astronomical number of years. For the next five years until the 'right person' comes along you can spend every day feeling discouraged and depressed, you can freak out at every engagement announcement that comes by, but guess what? At the end of that five years, when you're standing at the altar across from the man of your dreams, those five years of your life still existed. They existed if you cried every day. They existed if you lived a super-awesome life.

Freaking out does not speed up the outcome, it simply changes the way we spend our days. We don't know when we will find our spouse. It could be next week for all we know. If it *was* next week wouldn't it be a waste of our time to have spent these last days of singleness feeling anxious—feeling upset that we are single? Freaking out does not change anything. I know at first glance that's a super-annoying piece of advice. The reason we freak out is *because* nothing is changing, so re-emphasizing that fact doesn't seem like it's going to help. But think about it . . . that's the reality.

I know sometimes people have freak-out moments that look more like panic or anxiety attacks. That's a different story altogether, and those levels of panic may require more than simple logic to settle us down. The kind of freak-out moment I'm talking about is when I have let my mind trail down the long road of 'what ifs'. It's when I have allowed myself to stop and think on each scenario until I got myself worked up or miserable for the rest of the night. Right now, I am waiting. Do I want to be waiting? No. But do I have to wait? Yes. I have to wait if I am thrilled. I have to wait if I am ticked off.

When I heard that, I would think, *Yeah, I get it's pointless. But how do you **stop** freaking out?* For a start, by realizing how useless it is. I remember Joyce Meyer pointing this out in a message about worry where she said the first reason to not worry is that *it is totally useless.* Worry is useless. Freaking out is pointless. The Bible says:

"Who of you by worrying can add a single hour to your life? Since you cannot do this very little thing, why do you worry about the rest?"

Luke 12:25-26

What I can envision is that we will reach our destination, our romance, our wedding day, or whatever it is we are longing for, and look back and think, *It all turned out fine . . . I didn't need to spend so much time being upset.* Instead of waiting until the day when we'll look back and realize all our worrying was in vain, let's do it now. Ask God to give you the desires of your heart, and live like you are going to get them! Enjoy the 'right now'.

Remember, when you get caught up in all the 'what ifs' and freakout moments, just look at the step in front of you, *not* the whole staircase of your life. We spend so much time solving problems in our head that are not current problems. They might never be problems! Corrie Ten Boom, a woman who survived the holocaust once said, "Worry does not empty tomorrow of its sorrow. It empties today of its strength." How true! Move forward in strength. Move forward in joy. Focus on today, and walk in faith that your future will exceed your expectations.

7

Weeding out
the Thorns

HAVE YOU EVER SEEN one of those old-fashioned phones, maybe at your parents' or grandparents' house, which was attached to the wall by a cord? They could be so annoying, especially when the person you were calling put you on hold, because you could do nothing but stand there waiting until they came back on the line. You could walk about two feet in each direction, letting you clean up a few things around the kitchen, but that was as far as you could go. Otherwise, you just had to stand there and wait. You had some sort of mission to accomplish on your phone call, and until you got what you were looking for, you could do absolutely nothing else.

This is what I felt like waiting for a spouse. I had asked God for one. I was waiting for his answer. However, until he came through for me, my life was on hold. It was clear to me that marriage was the next step on my journey, the next chapter of my life. That is what I was waiting for. I needed to meet a man in order to move forward. But it wasn't happening. Like an old-fashioned phone call, everything was on hold and I was stuck waiting. I felt like I was pacing around in the same circle, day after day, taking a little step here or there, but going nowhere. I wanted to move forward, but I couldn't. I needed to meet a man in order to move forward, but I was still waiting for God to answer my request. Right now, I was on hold.

One week, when I was in church, the pastor preached about 'The Parable of the Sower'. It's a story Jesus told about a farmer who goes out and scatters seed in order to grow a crop. The seed is good and therefore should yield an amazing crop, but that's not what happens. Not all of the seeds produced an amazing crop. Some of the seed was eaten by birds, some fell into the cracks between the rocks, and some started to spring up but were choked by weeds and thorns. The only seed that produced a crop was the seed sown onto good, healthy soil.

I had heard this parable a hundred times, and you probably have too. But that week, the part of the story that hit me in a totally new way was the third scenario. In this scenario, good seed was sown and the plants were trying to grow, but their progress was stopped. This was not because something was *missing* in the environment. It was because of *the presence of something that didn't belong there*—the thorns. If they hadn't been choked by thorns, the plants would have grown beautifully. But because these thorns were thriving, any growth that was good was being choked out, and the young plants made no progress. This is how my life felt. I wanted to move forward and grow in my life, but something—some type of thorn of my own—was stopping my progress.

In Mark chapter four, Jesus explains what the thorns symbolize in our lives. In this story, the farmer sows 'the word', but,

> ". . . *the worries of this life, the deceitfulness of wealth and the desires for other things come in and choke the word making it unfruitful." (v. 19)*

The seed is the Word of God in our lives. The thorns represent the worries, desires and cares of this world. When the farmer planted the seed, the seed was good. A plant began to grow. But thorns quickly engulfed the little plant. They halted all growth and made the plants unfruitful.

This is what was happening in my life. My thorns—the overwhelming list of worries and desires—were taking away my life and halting all growth. I had the scriptures in my life, but anything God was trying to grow inside of me or through me was being stunted. I tried to pray more and tried to find faith and joy. I tried putting in more and more 'good seed', creating more of a chance for growth in my life, but it didn't work. The key to thriving was not in what I had to add, but in what I had to take away. *I needed to remove my thorns.*

If God was trying to direct me towards something (or someone), I was missing it. If he had plans for my life, I was missing them. If he was trying to bless me, or guide me, or use me, I was missing it. Yes, I asked for his guidance. I asked for his plan. But I was so focused on my own desires and my own plans that I wasn't leaving room for anything else to grow. If God was trying to lead me towards anything that *didn't* look like marriage, I wouldn't even know. I wasn't open to letting him write my next chapter in a new or different way. In *my* mind, marriage was next, so I never even considered that God might be trying to lead me any other way. Life felt like it was on hold, not because I couldn't find my marriage partner and move forward, but because of *my anxiety about finding a man.* It wasn't God who was 'putting me on hold' at all!

Thankfully, phone calls don't usually get placed on hold anymore—no one has time for that, and with today's technology, it's not necessary. Instead, we hear the option: "Would you like a call-back when we are ready?" "Yes!" I always select that 'call-back' option. Why would I want to sit with a phone to my ear waiting, when I could just live my life until I get the call? With God we have something like this kind of service available to us. We are free to live life without being confined by a *prayer in process.* It's not like he's going to forget what we want if we aren't sitting in one place tapping our foot. We can get off hold! We can select the option that allows us to live our lives freely and with enthusiasm. We can eagerly await the time when that phone rings ... when that prayer is answered ... when the time is right. But until then, why stand around, unwilling to move until God answers our specific prayer?

This realization brought a change for me. All of a sudden, a world of possibilities opened up. Now, if God placed an idea in my heart, I was willing to move towards it rather than disregard anything that wasn't marriage. Finding a man was not my next step. It was just the next step *I wanted.* I had told God it was what I wanted. What I needed to do now, however, was to begin to see my life as a beautiful story that God was unfolding moment by moment. I decided to be open to the idea that maybe marriage wasn't quite next on the list. What if he wanted me to do something else first? I didn't *want* to do other things first—that is what was holding me back. But I began to believe there were some 'other things' God wanted me to do. I finally knew I needed to take that strong desire to find a spouse, hand it to God, and open myself up to what else my next few months or even years of life could look like. This didn't mean I let go of wanting marriage. It just meant I decided to 'live life' until the day I met my man.

With that realization, my life started to change. Once I decided to open myself up to the possibility of God leading me towards other things, I began to notice little ideas that had been on my heart. During my struggles with being single I would often find encouragement in a quote or a passage of scripture and think, *It would be nice to share that with some other singles.* Sometimes it was just a passing thought, and sometimes I would imagine what it would be like to have a group chat of single girlfriends, or maybe start a blog. I believe now that God was gently nudging me towards something he wanted me to do in this season—encourage other singles. These small nudges kept popping up over and over. Eventually, this led me to begin writing a book on my experience of singleness and create an Instagram page to encourage other singles.

Saying to God, "I want a husband," only to feel like he was saying to me, "Write a book about that," is not necessarily what I wanted to hear. But the reality is, if I want to experience the blessings God has for me, they are going to come when I am walking on his path, not mine. If marriage is something God is planning for me and I follow his path for my life, that will be the path that my husband is on. I can try to create all these paths that lead directly to a husband, and if I could find a way to make it happen right now, I would. But honestly, in my pursuit of what I wanted, I was not being true to what I felt God was leading me to do. Was *my* next plan for my life to start an Instagram ministry and write a book? *Absolutely not!* It wasn't my plan, but I felt that was where God was leading me. I still desired marriage. But I was able to rest knowing that wherever I went next, if God was leading me there, it would be a blessed place.

Imagine a number of streams flowing into and through our life, each carrying our peace, our joy, our faith, the answers to our prayers, and gifts (or blessings) from God. In this analogy, let's swap out thorns for a tangled mass of dead leaves and branches caught up in the middle of each of these streams. These tangled masses hold back the flow of the streams. Like a dam wall, they hinder progress. These leaves and branches, like the thorns in the parable, are the cares of this world, our anxieties, our fears, and our distractions. We pile them up and wonder why it feels as though nothing is moving. Clearing these blockages lets the streams merge and flow as God intends. This means picking up our worries and cares, handing them over to God and continuing to move forward. We won't always know what to do next. And maybe for some of us, the next step *will* be meeting someone. However, it is not for us to try and figure out exactly how things will go. It is our job to ask God what he is leading us to do, whether that means dating a certain way, taking a new job, starting a Bible study, or something else we have felt quietly nudging our heart. I am not saying this will ensure you get all you want right away. It is more like pressing the play button on your life.

This time of singleness is often called a 'waiting season', but I believe that label is a poor description of what our lives should look like right now. We aren't in a waiting room, chilling until life begins. Life is happening right now. Get off hold, put down the 'phone', go out and live your life, and when it is time, you will get your man (or woman). Until then, don't allow yourself to be hooked to a cord that is tethered to a future occurrence. We've got cell phones now that will find us when our call comes in. If you're seeking God and want his will in your life, you are safe to explore the world. Safe to explore the passions he has put inside you. Safe to explore what new things you could take on next. God doesn't need you to stop living your life so you can be available for the moment you will come into contact with your man. Stop waiting on hold, and press the option that says, "Would you like a call back when we are ready?"

I believe marriage is a beautiful thing and it is beautiful that you want to experience it. The problem is when it becomes something we have to have so badly that we can't even live our lives in a thriving, growth-filled way. It is possible to want a spouse and still be living a life of abundance until you have one. If anxiety or worries seem to be keeping you stuck in place it is time to say, "No, I am not letting the thorns reach up and choke out my life. I refuse to spend my life on hold." You can have all the blessings of God in whatever season you are in right now.

So, what would I tell you to do? Live! Yes, get off hold. Start doing all the things you have been waiting around for. These can even be silly things. I remember saying to my friend Meghann once, "Oh I would like to put some cute shelves in my apartment and decorate them with plants and pictures, but I think it's kind of silly to spend money on decorations for my apartment since I don't plan to stay here long anyway." That statement that came from my hope that I would only be in the apartment another year or so—ya know, just until I found a husband. I didn't want to spend too much time or money making it fancy. But Meghann looked at me and replied, "Or . . . you could just live in the moment and decorate your apartment anyway."

As usual, that was some great advice from Meghann. Why would I keep myself from enjoying my home right now because of the anticipation of the next chapter of life? That is the definition of living life on hold. It is saying, "I'm not gonna do this now, since I plan to be married soon," or "I will wait until I am married to (fill in the blank)." You can do a lot of awesome things while you are married, but you can also do a lot of awesome things now. Why reject 'awesome' because you are waiting for what you believe will be 'even more awesome'? Can't you have both? This doesn't mean that you lose your hopes and dreams for the future, but it means that you stop letting your future dreams steal your present.

Ask yourself, "What sort of things am I interested in doing? What have I been waiting around for until I'm married?" For me these were things like, *My mattress is old and dips a little, but I'll wait until I'm married to buy a new one; then I can buy a king size.* Or I would hold off on getting household appliances since I could just wait until I put them on my wedding registry. But why does everything have to wait? Can only married people create homes, and decorate their living space, and vacuum with a nice vacuum cleaner? No. *You* can. If you're an adult, you can create an amazing life for yourself. Remember, you are not waiting for your spouse to complete your life or make it awesome. You are looking for a person to join in on your already awesome life and to create a new awesome life together! If you haven't been building your life, then get started. There is so much you can do.

What if you really 'lived' in this season of life rather than seeing it as a chunk of days, months, or years of just waiting for the next thing? Singleness is more than a waiting room. It is a full-on chapter of life. You want to be in another chapter, but while you are in this one, how can you make it amazing? How can you make it productive? How can you make it worthwhile? Those were some of the questions I asked myself. But the thing that helped me find the biggest answers was going back to my hypothetical 'five year' scenario. What if I have to wait another *five years?* What if, *five years from now,* I finally get what I want, and I am married to an amazing, godly man? At that point, I will have the answer to my prayer, and I will feel so excited. But how will I want to look back on the past five years of my life? Do I want to look back on five years of waiting in agony? Do I want to stand there with my dream man and think about how much life I wasted by worrying this moment would never happen?

The length of time is not what is important. What's important is to ask yourself *how* you want to be living your pre-married time. What will you want to look back on? What if you only have one more year of being single? What if it's only a few months? What if, and hopefully this won't happen, but what if it ends up being a way longer time than we want? When we get down the road and look back, what are we going to see? How will we spend this time?

Here is what I decided: If I'm not paying for a wedding right now, then I'm going on to do as many cool things as possible. If the perk of not having kids is that you have the freedom to do whatever you want, then I am jumping on that train and taking full advantage of it. Would I love to have a husband and kids? Yes. But I don't right now. What I *can* do is create a cool, thriving life, and take advantage of the benefits singleness has to offer, such as the ability to go on adventures just for fun without being neglectful of my responsibilities.

So that's what I did. I visited as many cool places as I could. I tried new foods, I spent a ton of time visiting my family, I became a better person, I grew in my spiritual life, I worked through emotional baggage I was carrying, I figured out who I was, I developed great friendships, I enjoyed my time alone, I allowed God to lead me into unexpected places and activities, I invested my money and got myself in a great financial situation, and I had so much fun doing it! I realized if that is what I wanted to look back on at the end of my wait, then that is what I had to create now. So I did.

I decided I wanted to see the world. I was no longer going to wait until I was married, and I was no longer going to wait until someone else's life aligned enough with mine to be available for a trip. I decided to just go. I googled safe places for women to travel alone. Iceland came up top of the list. I did more research and discovered it's the land of fire and ice, meaning there are geysers, lava, hot springs, glaciers, a beach with chunks of ice washed up that look like diamonds, and it's safe. I decided to stop thinking about it and just do it. I took a week off work, booked a flight, and announced to my family, "I'll be in Iceland if you want me!"

The fun part was that my sister suddenly said, "Wait, I want to go with you." So, she booked the same flight. Together we rented a campervan that allowed us to drive around the entire country wherever we wanted and then stop to sleep for the night. We explored glaciers, stopped to pet the friendly little Icelandic horses grazing on the sides of the road, soaked in a hot spring, and found waterfalls buried deep in the crevices of cliffs. Let me tell you, I had never even thought of doing something like this, but it was hands down one of the best experiences of my life so far. It would not have happened if I had not decided that

I was going to live in my 'now' and create an amazing life right where I'm standing.

I started a special savings account called 'my trip fund' where I would stash away cash for adventure. I booked other trips. Sometimes they were to visit my grandparents or see my friend who lives in another state. Other times, I went solo. Once I flew to Las Vegas, rented a car and drove five hours to San Diego. So many people asked the reason for my trip. I partly expected them to have pity on me when I told them I was on a solo trip, but the responses were just the opposite. "Wow, I seriously admire that!" or "This makes me want to go somewhere by myself." It was fun meeting new people and savoring the experience of exploring the world however I chose. It felt liberating. I was the one who got to write the chapter of my singleness, and this was definitely how I wanted to write it.

It was not all about trips. I also started exploring ways I could help other singles on this journey, since that was something pressing on my heart. I created an Instagram page to share what I was learning. I started going to counseling. I wanted to be healthy and find healing. I listened to lots of podcasts and audio books on topics such as dating, relationships, sexuality, and communication. These were areas I wanted to know more about. I wanted information that would help me now and later.

I hung pictures on my walls and decorated my living space just for me. I tried new foods whenever the chance came up. I exercised to mold my body, and read my Bible to mold my spirit. I visited my grandparents and had game nights with my family. I started reading some books to help me grow as a person, and other books just for fun. I went to see my favorite performers live, created dances with friends, and made fun little videos. I even wrote this book.

The point in giving you this list is not to tell you how to live your single life but to inspire you to go ahead and live it. If you listen to me talk and think, *Oh man, I haven't done anything exciting,* then let me tell you, that was me. I remember once talking to my friend about how people call marriage 'settling down' and I pointed out, "How can I settle down if I'm already settled down?" This was before I decided to embrace life. If you feel that you haven't done or experienced much, the great news is, you can start now. In fact, you *should* start now. What can you do to make single life more fun? What can you try, where can you go, what investments can you make? Don't just think about it—make it happen. I say this as a person who often dreamt about the things I would do 'someday' but learned that's the best way to make sure something never happens. I didn't stumble upon an Iceland adventure. I saved money, took time off from work, and booked a flight.

There will always be some reason why we think the future will be a better time to enjoy life. Maybe when we have more time, or more money, or we've hit a career goal. But your life is happening right now. Why not live it? What are you always saying you would like to do sometime or try some day? Do that. And if you need help thinking of things, just picture the future you with a spouse and kids and imagine the kind of memories you would love to look back on. What steps of growth would you wish you had taken? What opportunities would you wish you had savored? In what ways will you be glad you made yourself better? Do those. Now is the time to 'weed out the thorns' and begin taking bold steps towards an amazing life.

8

Sexuality in Abstinence

GROWING UP AS A typical 'good Christian girl', I knew the golden rule. Not the one that says, *Treat others the way you would like to be treated*. No, this rule seemed even more golden and was talked about way more. The rule? *Don't have sex until you're married*.

We read books about how to stay far away from boys so you wouldn't have sex. We learned rules like 'leave room for Jesus' (cue side hugs) so that we wouldn't even cause a boy to think of sex. We wore purity rings on our fingers—gold bands proudly worn as a symbol of our pledge of *no sex before marriage*.

The only thing we didn't talk about, was sex. Yes, believe it or not, we talked all about how damaging it could be, and how important it was to stay far away from it, and how to build an absolute cement wall of boundaries in our lives so sex couldn't possibly wiggle its way through. But we never talked about sex itself. We knew the basic mechanics of how Part A plugs into Part B, but what about all the steps leading up to that? What about the desire involved? I had about ten Christian girlfriends who were all in the same boat as me—zipped tight, saving ourselves for marriage—but none of us ever talked about sex. No one ever said, "Wow, this not getting to have sex thing, is a challenge!" No one ever referenced your sex drive, or what to do on a random Tuesday night when you felt turned on by a movie scene. No one mentioned words like 'fantasizing,' or 'masturbation'. It was all basically hush-hush. We didn't talk about it. We didn't learn about it. Yeah, of course we knew that sexual expression would be something totally awesome between a husband and wife . . . one day. But right now, if you weren't a husband and you weren't a wife, then sex was not for you.

While the church was very quiet on the topic, however, the world just kept getting louder and louder about all things sexual. I remember listening to the radio on my drive home one day and noticing the messages from the songs were purely sexual. One talked about the movement of someone's hands in a sexual encounter and the other was flat out requesting a girl to strip. In every advertisement, in every TV show and in every non-Christian conversation, sex (or even just a sexual reference of some sort) was the star of the show. The world seemed to scream, "You have to have sex, and you have to have it now, and if you don't, you're missing out because it's the most amazing thing ever."

Meanwhile the church just said, "Don't do that." Yeah, that wasn't very helpful. And as a growing teen I started to realize that even though the rule had been clear all along—don't have sex until you're married—the journey was anything but clear. I was also getting another message, and it was that 'good Christian girls' like me wouldn't even be drawn to sex like other people because essentially, sexuality was worldly, dirty, and perverted. Sexuality seemed worldly, dirty, and perverted. And it wasn't just the church, with their strong emphasis on purity, that passed out this message. It was the non-Christians around me too. The way they would send me these messages would be like this: they would talk about their sexual experiences and then someone would randomly interject and say something like, "Someone cover Bri's ears; she can't hear this!" or "Bri must be *so* uncomfortable right now."

Let's just say this, I wasn't uncomfortable with the concept of sex. In fact, I felt the opposite. I felt fascinated. I felt curious about sex and how it worked. I secretly wanted to watch the sexy scenes on TV, and I felt my body respond to attention from guys. I felt so sexually 'awake', and at the same time, I felt so much guilt for having this 'dirty' desire. How could I?! I was supposed to be a Christian. And from what I could understand, 'good Christian girls' had nothing to do with sexuality until they were married. In simple terms, I understood sex as a single equaled 'bad'.

This is where I fell into heaps of guilt because if sex equaled bad, at least for me as a single Christian, did that also mean that . . .

- *wanting to experience sex equaled bad?*

- *thinking about sex equaled bad?*

- *feeling sexual desires equaled bad?*

- *learning about sex equaled bad?*

The answer to all those questions is, *no!* This is where we need to make a distinction that I feel has been missed for a long time. God created sex as something beautiful. God also created our sexuality as something beautiful. We have received a lot of guidelines about keeping sex for marriage, which I believe is an awesome, healthy thing to do. However, we have also been taught to believe our sexual desires shouldn't show up until marriage either. But it doesn't work that way.

God created sex, and he created humans with a desire for it. Nothing he creates is bad. That sexual side of you that experiences sex drive, sexual curiosity and sexual excitement, is normal—even when you are not married. You were not created with a sexuality power switch that flips on once you get married. You don't say, "I do" and suddenly a flood of urges and desires overtake you that you have never experienced before. Those desires and urges that will cause you to be drawn to your spouse are here even now, in your singleness. Your sexuality is a part of you *now*, even when you aren't married. And that is okay. Not only is it okay, it is normal—God gave that desire to you.

The reason I'm pointing this out is because this has been a huge misconception in Christian communities, one that causes unmarried Christians to feel so much unnecessary shame. I see sweet, godly, pure, young women who have hearts of gold after Jesus who discover they have a sex drive, and although it is a God-given desire, they feel like they are dirty for having the desire. Trust me, I know, I was once that girl. I knew not to have sex before I was married, but the more the world openly showed off all things sexual, the more I realized that I actually wanted to experience my sexuality. I was curious about it. I picked up on the attractions and flirty tensions in my interactions with guys. I noticed how good it felt when men gave me attention in a sexual manner. I wondered what it would be like to have sex. I even sometimes thought, *I can't wait for this.* And then I felt dirty because "sex equals bad." Why did I want these things? Why was I thinking about these things? Why did I have this 'problem'?

But I wasn't dirty. I was a normal Christian girl who *felt* dirty because of a very wrong message—the message that said sexuality was a sin. What is the correct message? The correct message is that sex is a valuable gift from God that needs to be stewarded. To 'steward' something means to look after it and make thoughtful decisions about it. To steward our sexuality is to direct it, guide it, and make thoughtful decisions regarding it. Just like you need to tend to your relationships and your body in order to be healthy, your sexuality requires that you become aware of it, and that you direct and train your desire. It does not need to be wiped away or 'prayed away'. It doesn't need to be stuffed down, suppressed, or shamed. But it absolutely *can* be stewarded.

I have often heard people talk about stewardship in terms of money. If someone is a 'wise steward' of their money, that means they understand its value, and therefore make wise decisions about where they want it invested, how they want to save it, and what they would like to spend it on. They take responsibility for their money as a prized possession. I believe this is how we can think of our sexuality as well. It is a gift to us from God, and one that holds such beauty and value.

As stewards of our sexuality, we are the ones who manage and oversee the sex drive given to us. Ultimately, we make the choices of where we want to spend and save it. I think so often in the church we have had this idea that waiting until marriage means we should not have sexual desires before marriage. It doesn't. It simply means when those desires come up, we get to decide what actions we take with them. I love this scripture where the apostle Paul says:

> "Now to the unmarried and the widows I say: It is good
> for them to stay unmarried, as I do. But if they cannot
> control themselves, they should marry, for it is better to
> marry than to burn with passion."
>
> 1 Corinthians 7:8-9

Paul mentions *burning with passion*—because it is a real thing! We are not just robots who decided to save ourselves for marriage one day, and from that day forward we ate peaches and sipped tea and never had a passionate thought cross our mind. We are humans! We have emotions, hormones, desires and drives, just the same as every other human on this planet. The difference is in the decisions we make, not in the feelings or desires we have.

In this scripture, Paul is bringing up the fact that although there are some of us who are able to remain single and be absolutely at peace with that, which is great, there are others of us (probably most), who experience a 'burning passion' that is also completely normal. The part

I love most is that Paul does not condemn us for burning with passion. He doesn't say, "If you are unmarried and are burning with passion, repent immediately for you are a sinner and a defiled human." Instead, he gives us guidance to direct that desire into a committed marriage.

My fellow godly, good-hearted Christian girls, I want to tell you so clearly that your desire for sex is not a sinful desire. It is a pure, God-given desire that one day, when you are with your husband, you are going to be so grateful to have. Your sexuality, your desires for intimacy and your attraction to the opposite sex are beautiful, amazing, and natural. Yes, there are ways we can act on these urges that are not pleasing to God, or are not the best for us, but that cannot be simplified to mean our sexuality is a bad thing. I love the way Debra Fileta phrases it in her *Love and Relationships* podcast: "It's not the appetite we need to repress, it's how we feed that appetite, because how we feed it determines the course of our lives."

Now here's an important point to bring up so that what I'm saying does not get misinterpreted. I remember posting once on my Instagram page about how our sexual desire was normal, and an enthusiastic follower chimed in, "Yes, exactly! God gave us the desire and he wouldn't give us a desire and tell us not to act on it!" This guy was super-excited about the idea of God saying, "Do whatever you want!"

I understood his logic—that God gave us sexuality, so we should be free to do what we want with it. Here's the thing—technically, we are. We can make whatever sexual choices we want to make. I will admit that at first it sounds like having no limits or guidelines is a great idea. I remember listening to a group of girls once talking about how they were 'born into the church' but have since taken the 'freedom and fun' approach.

I don't know about you, but having sexual freedom and fun sounds kinda awesome, and like a lot less work. However, as I listened to them talk, it got interesting. One girl talked about the fun of hooking up with a guy for the first time. She then mentioned how that very guy stopped talking to her the day after, and how being rejected right after sharing herself in the most intimate way left her feeling so broken. Someone else was saying how a lot of times she went further than she wanted with guys because she knew the guys expected it and she wanted to be accepted. One girl agreed about just giving in and said that sometimes it was easier because then the guy would just leave you alone. Yes, these girls were celebrating sexual freedom, but I couldn't help but notice that these stories didn't sound very free or fun.

Listening to them, I couldn't help but feel like maybe this was the 'why' behind the instructions God gives us sexually. It's like a doctor giving a prescription to a patient with very clear guidelines that say, "Take one pill, twice a day, with food." The doctor isn't being a dictator. He isn't trying to control your life. And he is definitely not saying, "If you do take this in a way other than the way I prescribed, I am going to be so mad at you." No, the doctor uses his knowledge of the medication and all of its side effects and benefits to give you instructions on the usage that will be the most beneficial to you. If you mess it up and end up with some kind of system poisoning, guess who is going to help you fix it—the doctor. However, he will continually emphasize that you go back to his instructions for the maximum benefit.

This is how I believe God's instructions work as well. I don't believe he is trying to take away our freedom and fun. I don't believe he is trying to control our lives. I believe he uses his knowledge of sex, and the consequences and benefits of sexual decisions, to give us instructions on the most beneficial usage. He knows about things like STDs, and pregnancies that occur too early. He knows about the chemicals released in your brain during sex—the ones that bond you to another human in the deepest way. He knows about the pain that comes from breaking off a relationship after that bonding has occurred. He knows how hard it is to make wise relationship decisions for your future once sex has become involved. He sees the people who feel pressured, the people who feel shame, and the people who feel regret. God knows the complexities of sexual experiences in an even deeper way than we do. It is *because* of his love for us that he does not say, "I gave you this desire, so do whatever you want with it."

This is why I believe we are called to steward our sexuality. I believe God wants to share his wisdom with us, and desires for us to use our freedom to walk towards the decisions that truly benefit us most. Like the doctor, God is not mad at you when you make mistakes or decisions that go against his guidance. In fact, if you find yourself with regret, hurt, or unwanted consequences, guess who is going to help you through it? God. However, like the doctor, he will also continually point you back to the instructions so you gain maximum benefit.

9

Taking the Driver's Seat of Your Sex Drive

IF I HAD TO pick the most challenging part of my long singleness journey, it would be trying to find the answer to this question: "What the heck do I do with my sex drive?!" Yes, I've learned I don't have to get rid of those desires. I've learned that I don't have to be ashamed of them. I've come to a point where I can very confidently and freely say, "Yeah, this 'not having sex' thing is difficult!" But what am I supposed to do in this long wait?!

I remember I used to get annoyed when I read that scripture from 1 Corinthians 7:8-9 where Paul says that it's better to get married than to burn with passion. I wanted to write a letter back to him saying, "Paul, my friend, great advice. I'm so glad you mentioned that. But see, there's a little piece of your advice I need clarification on. I have the 'burning with passion' thing down pat. It's that second part, ya know, the 'just go get married' part, that I am struggling with. I appreciate your wisdom, but I'm stuck in the no-husband area right now, so you know what that means—that's right, the forest of passion is burning, and I don't even have a bucket of water to put it out. It's a growing wildfire at this point. So, yeah, any advice on *that* would be much appreciated. Send help. Thank you."

In no way do I believe I have all of the answers to this endlessly complex and nuanced question. However, I can share with you the things that I have learned after being at this for quite some time. One of the first questions we ask when it comes to sexuality and managing our desires is: *Where are the boundary lines?* Think of the challenges of navigating physical boundaries even within a dating relationship. What kind of touching is and is not allowed? What activities are okay leading up to sex? All of these are valid questions. And there are more. What about all those other words that we don't even mention? Fantasizing? Pornography? Masturbation? There are so many experiences we can come across and so little conversation about them, which leaves us asking, "Where are the lines in my singleness?"

If you have felt confusion over this question, you are not alone. Firstly, I will say this, we know that as Christians, we do not want to live in sin. So, if there is something we are already convinced is a sin or the Bible clearly points it out, then that's a great place to draw some lines. For example, pornography invites us into lusting after someone who is not married to us and does not belong to us. That's pretty clearly something God instructs us against. But what about the areas that are not talked about in the Bible at all? Or the areas where we simply do not know what to believe? How do you go about knowing where your boundaries should be? I love this verse:

> *"'I have the right to do anything,' you say—but not everything is beneficial. 'I have the right to do anything'—but I will not be mastered by anything."*
>
> *1 Corinthians 6:12*

In regard to sexual immorality, the question we are often asking is, "Is this a sin?" We want to know what we are and are not allowed to do.

However, when the answer to the 'sin question' doesn't seem clear, this scripture provides us with a different point of view. It doesn't focus on things being 'right or wrong'. Instead, it presents two helpful questions:

- *Is this beneficial?*

- *Am I being mastered by it?*

To be mastered by your sex drive means that your sex drive leads your decision making, or you have found yourself in an addiction where you can't seem to say no. This chapter is titled *Taking the Driver's Seat of Your Sex Drive* because ultimately, we need to be in control of our own desires and urges. We should be the masters of our desire, not slaves to it. In another version of the Bible, the same verse is worded this way:

> *"All things are lawful for me, but all things are not helpful. All things are lawful for me, but I will not be brought under the power of any."*
>
> 1 Corinthians 6:12, NKJV

The idea of being 'brought under the power' of my sex drive, where I feel like I just can't seem to stop, or where I feel as though I need a 'fix' or a 'high' in order to be okay, is not the place I want to live. Have you been there? I have. That is not a place of freedom and I believe that experiencing the true joy of sex means experiencing sexual freedom. Sexual freedom doesn't mean doing whatever we want. It means we are not slaves to our sexuality. It means we tell our sex drive what we will and will not do, rather than making choices based on our desires that are not ultimately in line with what we want to be doing.

This is where we can make 1 Corinthians 6:12 our mantra, *I will not be mastered by anything.* In whatever area you are seeking answers, it may help to ask, "Is this beneficial?" Often, the things we chase after sexually consume our time without really giving us anything in return. Sure, we might get the few minutes worth of 'good feelings', but what is being added to our life? Or consider this, *What is being taken away?* Is this consuming your time? Is it guiding your decision making? Is it leaving you with regret, shame, and secrets?

I cannot give you concrete answers on where all of your boundary lines should be set, but I have wrestled with these questions myself. Since we're in a period of so-called 'waiting', it is so satisfying to grab hold of whatever small tastes of sexual satisfaction we can. I cannot tell you what is 'lawful' beyond what the Bible says—that is between you and God. But if you are truly looking for where to draw the lines, a great place to start is by deciding to cut out anything that does not benefit your life, as well as anything that is dragging you down or holds more power over your decision making than you do. Here are some questions to ask if you are trying to determine if something is beneficial:

- *Is this the way I want to spend my time?*

- *Am I in control, or is my sex drive in control?*

- *Is this a habit I would want in a future marriage?*

I would love to give solid answers to questions about what is right or wrong, and what is beneficial or not beneficial, but I can't. A lot of the time the questions we are wrestling with are not clearly articulated in the Bible. Instead, we have to come to some conclusions by ourselves using discernment and wisdom.

Managing the Flame

I remember going to a church campfire with my friend Sarah. Sarah was thirty years old and had never been close to a campfire before. She had grown up in New York City surrounded by high-rise buildings and paved streets. She was the type of girl who always wore dresses and sparkly earrings. Anything involving a nature-wilderness-camping vibe was foreign to her. As Sarah stood beside the cozy campfire in her long, floral skirt that night, she was having a blast. Everyone else was just sitting enjoying the flames, but not this city girl. She would run off to collect sticks from all over the lawn to throw into the fire. Then she stood there, watching them being engulfed by the flames. She got so excited every time she threw something in and the flames leapt up, or poked a log and the fire started to grow—it almost became like an obsession! Every time she jostled a log or threw something new in, you could see her eyes light up over the excitement of watching the fire leap and spark. Eventually, the fire was getting so big that people started to comment, "Sarah, the goal isn't to keep this thing going all night . . . you should probably stop throwing things in there." It was getting hard to manage the flames!

This same thing applies to our 'burning with passion' that Paul refers to in 1 Corinthians 7:8-9. The human nature part of us loves the excitement that sexuality brings. This is why our culture loves all things 'sex'. We have sex in our movies, sex in our books, sex in our songs, sex in our advertisements—it's everywhere! This is because it's a pretty universal thing to be drawn to sexuality. These fascinations tickle our desires, like throwing sticks into a fire creates exciting leaps and sparks. We love the good feelings, and it makes sense—they can be *really* good feelings! Even though we enjoy this process there remains one thing that can be a total pain: our ever growing, and hard to manage—flame.

The only action that truly helps is to *stop feeding the flame*. It's true that whatever you feed, will grow. Just like Sarah's campfire wouldn't calm down until she stopped tossing in the sticks, our passion will be incredibly challenging to deal with if we keep feeding it.

At a conference I went to, a panel of people were talking, and one man was highlighting this very thing. For him, his struggle had been that he kept giving in to sex before he was married. He didn't want to, but what he described was one of those situations where his desire seemed to be more powerful than he was. His story stood out to me because I remember him saying that one thing that helped him was removing all things sexual from his lifestyle. Meaning, no more sexual music. No more sex scenes in films or TV. No more sexual content. At first, that sounded extreme, but when I really thought about what he was doing, it made sense. If his sex drive was, shall we say, a growing monster, how could he get it to stop growing? He had to stop giving it 'food'.

This concept of removing things that fed my desires was one I began to implement in my own life. I had felt plagued by my sex drive too. Marriage was not in sight, so carrying around this intense desire felt like slow torture. I had loved coming home and watching two or three episodes of my favorite TV show. It was one of those soap opera type shows where every other scene had someone passionately falling in love or running into a closet to have sex. Watching that show was not helping me feel less tortured by my sex-less life. I knew that for me, watching an episode while trying to master my sex drive was the equivalent of walking into a bakery while on a diet.

The key is, if you are on a diet, stay out of the bakery. You will still be capable of saying no inside the bakery, but it's going to be a lot harder. And don't walk in there just to look! You'll smell the fresh bread, see the glistening frosting, and you'll either end up ingesting 750 calories worth of regret, or you'll leave with a heightened awareness of all you're missing plus a craving that makes you miserable. This did not mean that watching my favorite TV show was a sin or that I judged other people who watched it. It meant that for me, it was causing me to face even more intense struggles. Getting free of the struggle felt more important than being entertained by it.

Now I want to be very clear right here; I am in no way trying to create a legalistic set of rules for you to follow. I am not saying that all entertainment of a sexual nature is sinful, or that every Christian needs to do this exact same thing. What I am saying is, if you struggle with stewarding your sexuality, cutting out things that spark your sexual desires can be very helpful, especially if these things are leading you into habits you regret or are simply inducing a craving that makes you miserable. This isn't about following a specific set of rules. It is about being kind to ourselves. For me, I found that if I didn't want my sex drive to keep growing, I had to stop feeding it.

Know Your 'Before'

When I was in college, I met a girl called Emily who was a recovering alcoholic, loved Jesus, and was very committed to never falling back into the drinking problem again. There was a winter dance going on at the school, and a lot of the girls from our campus Christian group had decided to go. I remember talking to Emily, who was a part of this friend group, and she told me she'd decided it was not the best idea for her to go. Even though she had successfully stopped drinking, she knew her past patterns well enough to recognize that walking into a party atmosphere where others were drinking might cause her to stumble and go backwards on all her progress. I really admired this about her, because it would have been so much easier and even more fun to just go to the dance with the other girls. The dance was not a wrong place to be, and the other girls who went had a fun night of dressing up and dancing with each other. But for Emily, it was a place of temptation. She knew that to be serious about her boundaries, she had to be serious about the situations she walked into.

This guideline applies to all areas of life. The best way to maintain a boundary is to stop putting yourself in situations that might entice you to cross it. You will still be capable of saying no, even if you are in situations that tempt you, but it's going to be a lot harder. You want to stop spending money on clothes? Which is going to work out better for you—staying out of the mall, or looking at racks of clothes hoping you can resist buying something?

- *Walking into parties is what comes before you make a decision to drink.*

- *Walking into a bakery comes before deciding to buy a dozen donuts and ruin your diet.*

- *Walking into the store is what comes before buying a bunch of new clothes.*

If you are serious about keeping your sexual boundaries, you need to be serious about chopping off whatever comes *before* you cross them.

What does your 'before' scenario look like? What weakens you? What situation do you get into that makes it hard to say no every single time? It is not enough to say, "I won't do . . . anymore." You have to stop putting yourself in the scenario that always comes *right before* you make that choice.

If you've been in the Bible-reading world for a while, you are probably familiar with a fairly graphic verse in Matthew chapter five. Even though it sounds slightly barbaric, there is a whole lot of wisdom in it—I mean, if Jesus said it, it's gotta be good!

"If your right eye causes you to stumble, gouge it out and throw it away. It is better for you to lose one part of your body than for your whole body to be thrown into hell. And if your right hand causes you to stumble, cut it off and throw it away. It is better for you to lose one part of your body than for your whole body to go into hell."

Matthew 5: 29-30

Does Jesus really want you to gouge your eyes out? No. But the point he is making is that no matter how valuable, fun, or beneficial something is in your life, if it causes you to stumble, get rid of it.

What scenarios do you find yourself in *before* you cross the line? Is it something you watch on TV? Hanging out in your bed? Sitting alone with your laptop? If you want an easier time saying no to the temptation, start saying no to the scenario that leads to the temptation.

Identify Your Needs

Is there something missing in your life right now that sexual experiences can provide for you? I can tell you that for a period of time in my life, my answer was most definitely *yes*. I was involved in a very long-lasting family crisis that drained all the energy out of me. I was stressed and overwhelmed. On top of it all, I felt like I couldn't get sex off my mind. I entertained inappropriate attention from men and felt almost obsessed with things of a sexual nature. Looking back, I realize that yes, some elements of my desire were just natural parts of being a hormonal sexual being. But during that period of time, sexual experiences were providing me with just about everything I was missing. Something like an imagined scenario in my mind was enough to offer me a temporary escape from the pain of reality.

Sex is fascinating, and as humans we are drawn to it. Sometimes it's that simple. Other times, when we fall into repetitive sexual habits, it is because there is something even deeper that we're looking for. This is important to identify.

- *Sometimes, it's fun and excitement when life is challenging and painful.*

- *Sometimes it's being desired and accepted when we've been misunderstood or overlooked.*

- *Sometimes it's intimacy when we are struggling to feel connected to people around us.*

- *Sometimes it's the feeling of being wanted when we have been rejected.*

- *Sometimes it's a reliable source of 'good feelings' when we don't have solid ways of coping with what's going on around us.*

Sex provides a temporary solution for this list of feelings. And this list could go on and on. Ask yourself what you are feeling when you slip up sexually. What do your sexual experiences provide that you are otherwise lacking?

As great as it is to stop falling into unhealthy or sinful patterns, if we get to the root of what we are truly searching for, we can work towards getting our deeper needs met in healthier, non-sexual ways. Instead of simply stopping sexual activity, try finding things you can replace it with that are fulfilling in healthy ways.

- *If you are lacking connection, is there a way you can meet new people, or draw closer to the people in your life?*

- *If you are lacking excitement, is there something new you could add to your life? What do you enjoy? What makes you come alive? Do more of that.*

- *If you are looking for escape, can you meet with a counselor to discuss better boundaries or ways of coping?*

The truth is, you can fight off the temptations that come up, and you can stop engaging in sexual habits. Using sexual experiences to help provide what you are lacking is like putting ointment on a severed leg. There may be a minor soothing effect, but there is no real healing. To stop your sexual habits is simply taking away the ointment. There is deeper healing work that needs to be done. Start small. What is something you feel is missing from your life? And what are some healthy ways you can begin to meet those needs? Be gracious towards yourself. Wanting to medicate your pain is normal, just as taking an interest in sex is normal. Know that God cares and understands the struggle you are going through. Look to him to help you make choices towards sexual freedom that are truly beneficial.

Here are some practical steps to take. Ask yourself where you believe lines need to be drawn in your life. This means you determine where you are going to say, "I don't want to go there sexually anymore." Write down the things you do not want to do because you feel they are displeasing to God, or because they have more control over your decisions than you do, or because they are not healthy or beneficial for you. Remember, you don't need to shame yourself for struggling with these things. *Your desire for sexual expression is beautiful.* You get to steward that gift by making decisions that are in line with your vision, values, and beliefs. *This is freedom.* Remember, God doesn't condemn you. He invites you to experience true sexual freedom where you are not a slave to your desires. When you stumble, he still loves you and wants to guide you back into making healthy decisions.

What are the 'somethings' that feed your desire? What are the situations that come up just before you stumble? Once you identify the answers you can identify where more lines need to be drawn. You don't want to just say, "I won't fall into the same habit." You want to say, "I will get rid of *situations* that repeatedly lead me towards the same habits." Now ask yourself what it is you are needing right now? What things are you missing in your life? Identify these areas of struggle or hurt and brainstorm some healthy ways you can tend to your needs.

Above all, give yourself grace. Sexuality is a part of being human, and knowing how to navigate such a powerful gift can be challenging.

Know that God is on your team to help and guide you. He will be right there if you fall, and he will lead you in the direction you want to go. You are the master of your sex drive. Let God help you discover how to master it well.

10

Opening Your
Mind to 'How'

GUESS WHAT? I MET someone! I, the girl who felt so lost in singleness that she has written a whole book on it, have met someone worthy of transitioning from single to dating, to a committed relationship. Boy, is this a plot twist! Let me tell you, I am the author of this book and even I didn't see this chapter coming, at least, not yet. I had been writing for what seems like years—completely and utterly single. I would experience a struggle in real time, make an encouraging discovery, and think to myself, *I need to include that in my book,* then proceed to write a chapter.

When I began writing, I knew I wanted to include a chapter about dating. Dating is the inevitable step between singleness and marriage. Now that I have entered a relationship, I figured the best thing to do would be to share from that journey. You know what that means? My dating experiences are super fresh. Just as I could share my reflections about singleness as someone living it out in real time, I can now share the journey of transitioning from singleness to a relationship.

Also, a little clarification here: I am not engaged, and I am not married. I am in a relationship with a whole lot of potential. However, I don't know what is going to happen next. I think it is important to include this, because this phase of not quite being single but still not quite being married is a real part of the journey. We often talk about meeting our 'spouse', but the reality is, we don't meet a spouse. We meet a person, often a stranger, then date them, and over time learn if they will become our spouse. This transition phase is not discussed very often, but it has shown me some things that I want to share with you—what I have learned by walking the path of potential marriage, and what I am reflecting on from my period of complete singleness.

~

If you're anything like me, though, the question you're really wanting to ask is, "How did you meet?" This was always the first question to pop into my mind any time I heard of a single Christian finding love. This is partly because I love a cute meeting story. The other part of me was dying to know, *How did you do it? Tell me your story!*—because I wanted to find the secret!

Maybe this is only me? Either way, as much as I would love to pass along a secret tactic, I don't believe one exists. What I have found are a bunch of little things that I believe played a big role in finding this awesome man. Okay, okay. So let me answer the question. *How did we meet?* I had done lots of dating. Dating apps—so many dating apps. Blind dates. Singles groups. Church functions. You get the idea. I was basically putting myself anywhere and everywhere to meet someone. The crazy part? I didn't end up meeting him any of these ways. Now don't get me wrong, those are fantastic places for meeting someone. That just wasn't my story.

Instead, as I was trying to navigate life, I began to realize that I had certain strengths and I wanted to find a way to use them. I knew there were lessons I was learning in my singleness, and I felt the thought pop into my mind over and over, *How I can share this with other people? Maybe I could have a blog? Or an inspirational text group with my friends?* One of the ideas that seemed to keep coming up was starting an Instagram page to inspire others in their singleness. This seemed like a scary and uncomfortable venture. If I posted videos, would people actually watch them? That would be a lot of attention for my typically introverted self, but I didn't want to miss anything God was trying to do with me.

With this thought, I started an Instagram page. I posted multiple times a month for a year. I responded to DMs about singleness, I did Q&A in my Instagram stories. Then one day I received a video message from a stranger on the internet. I didn't open it at first, because like I said, it was 'a stranger on the internet'. Eventually I did open the DM. It was from a Christian man who had taken note of what I was doing, liked it, and decided to send me a message.

Later, I found out he had come across my Instagram page because he was intentionally seeking out a godly woman. One of his ideas was to search for Christian dating pages and look at the comments section of the posts. Pretty clever, huh? He saw a comment I had posted, checked out my page, and made the bold move of recording a video message where he introduced himself and asked me on a virtual date.

That's my little meeting story.

I can't say I've heard a story like this from any other couple, but that's just the thing—no one has the exact same story as any other couple. Each of us is an individual. Each of our stories is a unique story. Yes, many couples may say they met at church or on a dating app, but even then, the specific details are all unique to that couple. I say this because sometimes I think we are busy looking for that 'secret'. When we hear a successful story, we try to pull the 'how to' messages from it.

Ironically, I was on a short dating break when I received that DM. You could respond with, *See, it always happens when you finally stop looking.*

But then wait a minute. What about his side of the story? Reflecting on that, you could say, *See, it only happens if you're putting in the effort.*

Some Christians swing one way and say, "Leave it all to God—don't even think about a spouse!" while the other team yells, "If you want something you have to go after it." The problem is, both of these are over-generalizations. These statements try to pinpoint one method as 'the way' to meet someone. But what is being missed is that fact that there is not one way—there are endless ways, especially when we are partnering with God. There is no 'one secret method' God uses to get things accomplished. He can use anything.

God can use anything.

This leads me to the first piece of advice: Be open with your 'how' when it comes to meeting people. So many of us have prayed things like, "God do things beyond my imagination," but then we approach our dating lives by only taking steps that fit *within* our imagination.

For example, I remember chatting with one girl who said, "I wouldn't want to meet someone through DMs. It doesn't take as much boldness for a man as it does for him to come up to me in person. It works for other people, but that's not my style." She had decided that any version of online dating or messaging through social media was not how she would meet her future husband. I was thinking, "Wait a minute. If I had followed that rule, I wouldn't be in the relationship I'm in now." This made me wonder if sometimes we are telling God to move, but then limiting him with our own rules for *how* he can move. If we will only take steps that fit within our ideas, we don't allow room for God's ideas.

Another example comes from my own life. I remember attending a young women's gathering at church a few years ago. One of the girls messaged me after saying, "It was so nice to meet you! I think you and my brother would be great together. Can I set you up on a blind date?"

My initial response was, "No, I don't do blind dates." That is, until my mom responded, "Why don't you just go and see what happens?" Honestly, until my mom suggested it, I hadn't thought of saying yes. I just shut down that opportunity like I had shut down every other one. I decided to say yes, and even ended up in a short-term relationship with that man.

Even though I didn't end up marrying him, this experience taught me to be more open to doing things that feel uncomfortable because you never know what the outcome will be. I had originally been so focused on how uncomfortable a blind date sounded, that I overlooked the possibility of meeting someone I might actually enjoy spending time with.

Do you have specific guidelines for how you are willing to meet people? Have you decided there are certain ways that are unromantic, less spiritual, or simply won't work? The 'old me' had a very clear idea of how God would bring someone into my life. Thankfully, the newer version of me began to embrace opportunities to meet people. I began signing up for dating apps, going to events that had other singles in the mix, joining Bible studies, and trying different churches. I started hanging out at places outside my comfortable living room, and having conversations with new and different people. None of these ended up being the way I found the relationship I am in now. However, through this process, I had made a crucial mind shift. Instead of sitting waiting for something to happen in my dating life, I began stepping towards meeting people, and I began saying yes to things that were different and new.

If I hadn't shifted my mind into a place of being more open with how I met people, I may not have even considered responding to the guy who I now playfully refer to as "the dude from the internet." It didn't happen naturally as we were out and about in our usual lives. It took him searching and sending a message, and it took me deciding to respond to a guy I had never even met. It took both of us being willing to get to know someone who lived four hours away, and who had no mutual friends. It took both of us being open to something new and uncertain.

Another dating idea that may hinder us from really stepping out is, "You don't want to do God's job." Have you ever thought about this? The concern is that we don't want to take matters into our own hands and therefore out of God's. We want to let him work. I have totally believed this in the past, but let me share why my thoughts on it have changed a little.

I believe that living as a human being means we pair the natural with the supernatural. We have a supernatural God who moves in our lives. At the same time, we are created with free will and the ability to make decisions. We can fall into one extreme or the other. Either we do absolutely nothing, leaving it all up to God to supernaturally bring a marriage partner to us, or we go to such a big effort to make something work that we forget to include God altogether. The beauty lies in the balance. What if we step forward towards what we desire *and* seek God's guidance every step of the way? This doesn't mean we always know what step to take before we take it. Sometimes this means trying something new or trying something we just aren't sure of.

This balance becomes much more apparent when we look at scenarios outside of dating. For instance, my friend Sarah, who I've mentioned before, is a doctor at a prestigious hospital. She knew her whole life she wanted to be a doctor, so when the time came, she started applying to medical schools. She took tests, she studied hard, she dressed her best and went off to interviews. Sometimes she was applying to schools she wanted really badly, other times she was just exploring every opportunity available to see what would happen. In all of this, she prayed for God's guidance and clarity. She prayed he would open the doors that he wanted her to walk through and close the ones he didn't. She prayed over every interaction. She prayed, and she walked towards what she was praying for. It would have seemed crazy if we'd told her, "Sarah, don't apply to medical schools. You don't want to play God. Don't do anything, just live your regular routine and trust that God will make you a doctor." I think we all know it doesn't work that way. It would also be unwise for her to strive to become a doctor without involving God at all. It's the balance of the two that leads to the desired outcome.

This is the same balance I wanted in my dating life. Many people told me that trying to meet a man was me trying to be in control. I didn't believe that. Instead, I believed that putting myself out there and intentionally trying to meet other singles meant I was doing my part—opening doors of possibility. I also believed that God would do his part—connecting me with the right people.

Are there ways you could open some more doors in your dating life? Are you still holding onto guidelines for meeting someone that feel the most comfortable? Have you been holding yourself back from finding new ways of interacting with other singles out of a fear of doing something that is meant for God to do? Or are you putting yourself in situations where other singles have the opportunity to meet you? Are you having conversations with people of the opposite sex? If not, are there ways you can put yourself in these situations? Maybe try a new church? Maybe see what happens with a dating app? Maybe go to some social events near you?

And then . . . this is the best part . . . leave the outcome to God. Our job is to open the doors. Our job is to talk to people. Our job is to take hold of the opportunity to get to know someone or go on a date. As we connect with others and form relationships, God will guide us into the next steps. He will lead our relationships. We don't have to try and force them—we just have to walk towards what we want and see what God does. The story of God leading you to your spouse will be unique. Sometimes trusting God looks like stepping forward into the unknown, the new, and the different, and truly believing that he will direct you in the process.

11

Opening Your Mind to 'Who'

HAVE YOU EVER WRITTEN a list of the things you want in your future marriage partner? I have, and the list included over fifty items. It covered everything from physical qualities to personality traits, to hobbies and the exact age range. Talk about specific!

I also envisioned what it would be like to be with this dream man. I would think about it as I went through life, observing the way men acted. If someone did something tender in a movie, I would envision that as how my husband would be. He would have the style and class of the charming man in the musical, the sex appeal of Thor, and the career of the guy who takes the girl on exotic vacations. He would be as funny as the influencer on Instagram, and as well-spoken as the husband speaking on my morning podcast.

Alice, in *Alice in Wonderland*, frequently says, "Well in *my* world . . ." then follows through with a perfect vision of how she would like things to be. Her world is a specific one, different from the one normal people live in. I know I had a vision for my perfect spouse that fit in beautifully with 'my' world. The problems came when I started to compare each man I met to the ideal one I had crafted in my head. This dating method is one we often use and it can cause us to eliminate amazing people who are a part of the, let's just call it, 'real world'.

There is nothing wrong with desiring certain traits in your future marriage partner, and there is nothing wrong with dreaming about them. We have to remember, however, that real people come with so many remarkable traits, and at the same time they may not quite match our fantasy. We often create a dating obstacle for ourselves when we use our fantasy as our filter. This means we have an idea in our heads of what our spouse will look like and how they will act. Then we begin to search for that perfect ideal and scan right over anyone who doesn't match. No matter who we are dating, there will always be areas that don't perfectly match our ideal. This is because we are dating a human being, not designing a computer avatar. Only when we set aside our predetermined criteria can we begin to focus on all the traits the person in front of us has to offer. Often the first step in finding a relationship is breaking up with the relationship you hold in your imagination.

Let me be clear, this does not mean you should lower your standards. Don't ever let someone's positive traits override disrespect or poor treatment towards you. You should have a very clear set of standards established. I am pointing out that oftentimes we are not clear on what is a 'standard' and what is a 'preference'. Our standards should be our non-negotiables. This is the list of must-haves that are required to build a healthy relationship.

A lot of the time, however, we filter people out based not on our standards, but on our preferences. These details can be fun, or even feel important, but if we cling to them as though they are 'needs' instead of 'wants' then we can end up eliminating potential amazing partners in order to make sure we aren't missing out on any of the awesome traits we have envisioned in our heads.

If you are like me and have created your wish list, it may be time to toss that list out. This time, create for yourself a list of standards only. This list is significantly shorter and should probably only be around five items long at most. By doing this, you are better able to separate your *standards* from the never-ending list of *preferences*. This will help you avoid the trap of using your preferences to guide you and stay focused on the list of things you need in order to build a healthy relationship. Your standards will be specific to you, but here are mine. I want my potential husband to:

- *have a personal relationship with God that impacts his life and decision-making.*

- *have a growth mindset, be open to hearing feedback, seek out wise counsel, and be able to self-reflect and adjust his actions accordingly.*

- *feel mutual attraction and understand that attraction can take time to grow as we get to know each other.*

- *desire a family.*

- *seek to be a wise steward of finances.*

If you have ever had a fifty-point list like I did, this brief list of non-negotiables may seem over-simplified. With standards though, you are aiming to define your criteria for the foundation of a healthy relationship. Each of these foundational items encompasses so much more under the surface. For example, I believe that if a man genuinely loves God, then the way he treats me will follow suit. If a man is open to seeking counsel and gaining understanding, he can grow in problem areas that come up. If he is open to input and self-reflection, and I can communicate with him, then we can work through inevitable areas of conflict. In other words, define the criteria needed for building a foundation of relational health. All other areas, like details of his or her style or what he or she does for fun, are minor details that don't truly impact the quality of the relationship.

I found that when I drifted from my standards and assessed people based on my preferences, I created a huge barrier to entering a relationship. I was trying to find a great match but analyzing all of the wrong things. Because of this, it would have been easy to have a great man standing right in front of me and to completely miss him.

If we want God to work beyond our imagination, we have to stop limiting him to scenarios we can imagine. We can't pray for God to give us a healthy relationship, but turn down every person who is too young, too bald, too short, or too shy.

Would you allow God to bring you the love of your life if the packaging was different? This used to be a scary thought for me. I felt that if I let go of what I wanted, I would end up disappointed. Releasing your preferences does not mean you have to marry someone you don't find attractive or you don't enjoy being around. It simply means you don't allow your fantasy to become your filter. Look beyond your list of preferences. You don't need to settle, but you do need to remember that in your fantasies you are creating perfection, and perfection doesn't exist.

When you let go of your own ideas of what will make a great marriage partner and begin to date openly, you let God show you the beauty of stepping outside of what *you* think is best. One hundred miles was the distance radius I always set on my dating apps. That meant one hundred miles was as far as I wanted to travel to connect with someone. I could have told you all the reasons why a long-distance relationship just 'wouldn't work for me' and why I needed to keep the driving time to an hour and a half maximum. Well, low and behold, 'the dude from the internet' didn't conveniently live within those one hundred miles. He lived a solid four-plus hours away. I don't think even he knew how far 'upstate' I meant when I said I lived in upstate New York. Honestly though, as it turned out, that was probably for the best. Had we known the distance, it might have been a quick write-off for either one of us. Traveling that far was not on our list of preferences, but getting to know each other across a significant distance gap created a pretty unique experience.

Dating from a distance can have its downsides, but I discovered that by 'allowing' our distance apart, I got to observe how he filled it. For example, one day he drove an eight hour round trip just to take me to dinner. This gesture made me feel so valued, and created a very special experience. I began to get excited for our nightly phone calls and realized that our time apart actually made our time together feel so sweet. Would it have been more convenient to have a boyfriend who lived down the street? Yup. But distance created unique and beautiful experiences that I wouldn't have had otherwise.

The point here is not that long-distance dating is better or that driving miles and miles is the only way you can easily discover someone's intentions. The point is that I saw standards in him that felt right to me. I had decided what I needed in a person. I had determined what I felt was important. As I began to release my grip and stop holding so tightly to each of my preferences, I was able to see how much beauty existed outside of them.

Is it possible that your ideas for what makes a great life partner are limiting you as well? Maybe you only say yes to a certain 'type'. Maybe you are holding on to ideas like, 'the man can't be younger than the woman', or 'I need someone who is super-strong so I feel safe'. Could you be saying no to something great simply because he or she is different from what you have imagined? You have the option to hold tightly to what you want, or to allow God to show you what you really need. Will you allow him to give you 'different' so you can experience 'better'? We can try to paint the picture of our own lives, yet when we hand the brushes over to God we begin to see what appear to be splotches on our perfect canvas. This is how he begins his masterpiece.

It felt scary to date my new boyfriend. On the one hand I could see how he exhibited the standards I desired. On the other hand, he had many traits that were different from those I had imagined—not bad, just different. I remember thinking early on, *I just don't know.* This was a new experience for me because with most of the guys I had dated, I did know the answer. I knew they were a 'no' within the first few dates. Sometimes it was a strong 'no', like with the guy who told me he gets buzzed every night. Other times it was simply a dead end to conversation. In these scenarios the answer was clear. Even though the repetition of no's felt exhausting, the fact that I had certainty about the decision gave me clarity. But with this man, I didn't see a definite 'no' when I looked at him.

That may sound exciting. To me, it was unsettling. I didn't have a 'no', but I didn't have a definitive 'yes' either. I remember one night I felt tons of anxiety and began to explain it to him on the phone. He asked me for clarification: "What are you afraid of?" I told him that this felt like a risk. What if I started to get more emotionally involved and found out it wasn't right? I didn't want to get hurt. I didn't want to hurt him. I just wanted answers, confirmation. But as much as I tried to grasp for solid answers in my head, I just couldn't.

He very calmly told me, "This is what we're going to do. Open your Bible to Proverbs, chapter three, and read verses five to six." I read out loud:

"Trust in the Lord with all your heart and lean not on your own understanding; in all your ways submit to him and he will make your paths straight."

This was such a great reminder for me. Trying to lean on my own understanding was leaving me so confused. My brain wanted to figure it all out. However, what I needed was to ask God for his help and continue to step forward while trusting he would guide me. Sometimes stepping into risk is the only way to grab hold of the beautiful reward at the end. Often we don't know until we try.

Since then, Proverbs 3:5-6 became *our scripture*. Most couples have a song, we have a scripture. But the point is this: No matter what the season, no matter what you are facing, do you actually trust the Lord? Trusting God doesn't necessarily mean you always remain within the bounds of 'safety' and familiarity. It sometimes means stepping into the unknown.

One of the biggest lessons I have learned is this: Take the risk. Risk can feel so scary, but if you stay where you are certain of the outcome, you may miss out on the reward. If you stay where you're safe and secure, the concept of trust is irrelevant. You don't need to trust anyone else when you are in control. It's when you take a risk . . . when you step into the unknown . . . when you try the scary thing . . . when you do something you don't feel ready for, that trust in God comes to life. Can you surrender your own understanding? Are you willing to take a risk and rely on him to direct your paths? These are the questions I had to ask myself.

Let me remind you of this when you face your emotional reaction to taking a risk: God did not bring you this far in life to leave you now. If you seek him, he will direct you. This means you can take steps forward in the face of uncertainty and leave the outcome to a God who is certain. You can be at peace even while there are no answers because you have a God who has the answers.

It's important to be aware that building a relationship is a process. When our mind envisions meeting 'the one', we often imagine that we will just 'know' whether a person is right for us or not. The reality is that relationships involve a process of learning about a person and evaluating them. Reality may include doubts, fears, questions, and uncertainty. It will include things you love about the person and things you don't really like. It will include things that make you smile and things that you're not sure you want to deal with for the long term. It's easy to feel like this process shouldn't have to happen. We often believe that if it's the right fit, we will just 'know'. The truth is, that building a relationship takes two people being willing to get to know each other and work together.

One last thought: while I was single, I spent a lot of time looking at my current situation and thinking it was an indication of my future. I worried that the standards I held meant I wouldn't be able to find someone. I worried that I wouldn't get the experience of being in a godly relationship. I sometimes felt that I would have to choose between lowering my standards and being single.

Although I don't yet have a guarantee of where my current relationship will lead, just by walking through this experience I can say those thoughts were not the truth. There are, in fact, singles out there who hold high standards just like you. Godly singles exist. Good relationships exist. And yes, they even exist for people who once felt their chance of finding someone was nearly impossible. If you feel this way now, I hope my experience is a reminder to you that fearing something does not mean it is true. Hold on to hope for your future because what seems impossible to us is possible with God!

12

Looking
Back

"Now that you're in a relationship, would you have done anything differently in your singleness? When you look back, what are the things you're glad you did?"

I was recently asked these questions and they were amazingly thought-provoking. It's funny to think about it because I haven't been in a relationship all that long, so I wouldn't consider myself an expert. I haven't forgotten the struggles of singleness—not even one bit. The cool thing is though, I have stepped outside of it enough to look at it from a different viewpoint. As a person who is currently in a relationship, navigating its joys and challenges, *What would I tell my single self to do to prepare for this stage? What would I do if I were to go back to being single?* These are great reflective questions that I've spent time thinking about. Here are some tips and ideas:

Savor the Adventure and the Ordinary

This is something I did well in my singleness, and I'm glad I can look back and say I learned to enjoy life. I found appreciation in the ordinary and excitement in the adventures. My advice? Wherever you live, make it yours no matter how long you plan to live there. Decorate the apartment, the bedroom, or the dorm. Heck, if you can, even buy the house. Get dressed up and look pretty just for the sake of feeling pretty. Spend time with your family and whoever it is you love the most. Shared experiences are priceless. Loved ones are priceless. Once you're in a relationship, time gets divided, the place you live may change, and priorities may rearrange themselves. However, in singleness you can spend your time wherever you please. Do it.

See the world—but not just the world far away. See *all* of the world, even the simple things right where you are. Try the strange food. Take a class in dance, go rock climbing, or find a group to go bowling with. Don't think you'd be good at any of those things? Who cares? Make life an adventure worth experiencing. There is comfort in the usual but there is adventure in something new. Choose intentionally to experience both—because you can. Take a hike near you. Go on a solo trip or ask everyone you know to go with you until someone says yes. Take the window seat on a plane and look out. Stay up past bedtime. Grow some plants.

The key here is that you have to take action, not just think about doing these things. This can be the most challenging part, I know. But do it. You will be so glad you did. I can now look back and think, *Wow, that was a really great season of life.* Did you ever hear someone refer to 'making memories'? Memories don't just happen—you have to make them. Make your life amazing, because it absolutely can be, single or not. You can't control your life, but you can control how you live today. What new things can you try? What ordinary things can you find a fresh appreciation for? Write them all down. Make them happen. Savor every minute you can.

Clarify Your Purpose

Do the things God puts on your heart. The purpose you have right now is bigger than waiting-for-a-relationship-to-happen. I know this one can seem obscure. Do you want to walk in your purpose but don't know where to start? Use your gifts. Do what you're naturally good at. Are you good at talking? Writing? Art? Are you good at encouraging? Find ways of encouraging people. Are you a helper? Then help. Look for the talents God has placed in you. What can you do with those gifts? It doesn't have to be profound. There is beauty in doing things God gave you the ability to do even in ways that feel small. Using my gifts to benefit others really helped me as a single person. I loved the feeling of knowing I was using my days for good and that they were not being wasted. I felt like I had found what I was meant to do.

Is there something you've often thought about doing but you still aren't sure where to start? Regardless of the outcome, regardless of success or failure, and regardless of what blessings may await you, *use this time*. Find those things, those little sparks in you. Begin to use them in whatever way you can think. Even if it feels sloppy, doing something imperfect with your gifts is better than not using them at all. You don't have to search for some big, mysterious purpose. Just do what you're good at. If you're unsure of where to start, start somewhere small. You don't have to see the whole picture, but move forward and let God lead the outcome. The reward of stepping out in boldness is way better than the security of staying hidden.

The key is to just get started wherever you are. For example, have you always felt a desire to lead a Bible study? Start one, even if it's just you and a friend. I had struggled with being single, as you already know, and I've mentioned those ideas that came to mind about ways I could encourage other Christian singles. When I stopped thinking about this and decided to do it, I felt so unprepared. My Instagram profile was a small, unprofessional looking page with fifteen followers—my family and friends. I pieced together a video that took me hours to make. I was terrified of people seeing that video because I felt embarrassed. But I kept going, and slowly my following grew.

I moved forward with my singles ministry for two reasons. The first was, *What if it was God who was giving me the gentle nudges in this direction?* If that was the case, I didn't want to ignore something he was leading me into. I didn't want fear or discomfort to stop me from doing something God wanted. I wanted his plan, and I wanted his blessings. Even though I felt completely unsure how to move forward, I just kept going. The second thought was, *Even if just one person benefits from me doing this, it's worth it.* This helped me not to focus on the numbers. Instead, I openly shared the things I had to offer as if I was speaking to one person.

Behind the scenes, I began writing this book, but I was afraid to tell people because I felt clueless as to what I was doing. Those words, "I'm writing a book," felt so uncomfortable coming out of my mouth. But I still had that tiny little spark alive in me—so I kept going. I wrote the book.

Finding a sweet, awesome man through my Instagram page, that 'dude from the internet', was amazing. In fact, this part really blows my mind—all those years of praying for God to send me a man when it felt like the only guidance I was getting was to *go help other singles.* Then how God gave me the ideas to start a ministry. How that ministry helped others. How that ministry gave me a sense of purpose in my waiting. And how that ministry led me to meet a man I would not otherwise have ever met. This is not a lesson on how to find a spouse. It's just a great reminder that the blessings God has for us are right there, along the path he is leading us down.

Pursue Growth

When I think back, I am so thankful I used my time of singleness to invest in growing as a person. I can see how the growth that happened in my singleness is impacting the relationship I am now in. The younger Brianna was the girl who had experienced toxic family situations and witnessed abuse but was afraid to speak up, never said what she wanted, believed things simply because she was told, thought conflict was bad, played it safe, and always picked the more familiar route. Your situation will be different, but we all have areas where we can grow, improve, or heal.

The Bible tells us to seek wisdom and godly counsel. I read books, listened to podcasts, found a good therapist, and had many discussions with wise friends who built me up. The important part is *seeking out* wisdom for your life and habits in whatever form you can. To listen to an audiobook while you go somewhere in the car takes no additional driving time. To meet with a therapist once or twice a month takes a little additional time, but it's worth it.

Counseling is one of those things that people don't always talk about. It is not just reserved for people who feel like they have serious problems or trauma, although if you do, then counseling is an amazing tool. It is for everyone. Everyone can benefit from talking to a counselor, therapist, or mentor about ways you can improve your life. Our communication style, habits, thought patterns—these are all areas where we can constantly grow. As someone who is currently in the 'girlfriend' role, I can see where my relationship is healthier because of what I was doing even before I got here. I am so thankful for this. Relationships take work, but working on yourself even before entering a relationship means there is less you have to sort out once there is another person in the mix.

Pour into your spiritual life by talking to God about what is on your heart. Develop habits that help you check in with God throughout your day, like reading your Bible and praying. I didn't always do the best in this area while I was single. I was often so focused on my lack of relationship with another person that I neglected my relationship with God. He was still there though. In both singleness and relationship, I can see how much of a difference it makes when I draw close to God. It changes my perspective, my peace, and my clarity.

Grow towards where you want to be financially. Create a savings account, start investments, take the promotions, pay off your debts. There are so many areas where we can work towards becoming healthier—emotionally, mentally, physically, spiritually, sexually, and financially. The healthier we become in our singleness, the healthier our relationships will be. We don't need to get healthy in order to *earn* a relationship. Our growth enhances our own lives, and the great thing about becoming healthy right now is that we are simultaneously working on the health of our future relationships.

Let me tell you, being in a relationship does not look like meeting your Prince Charming, finding that both of you are perfectly on the same page, and suddenly all your problems are solved. It looks more like facing a whole new set of challenges as you try to partner with another human being with all their likes, interests, and views. Now I can see how beneficial it was to spend my singleness growing and becoming healthier. This is not to say that you have to reach some 'level' of health before you can be in a relationship. There is no finish line for growth. The important part is that today you are investing in becoming even stronger and healthier than you were yesterday. This is something that will benefit you no matter what season you are in.

Balance Dating with Living

This one can be hard. There were times when I wanted to meet someone so badly that I used so many apps and went on so many dates to the point where it was consuming all my time. That wasn't necessarily bad, although I ultimately felt like I was missing out on life. I wanted to do things that excited and interested me, not just continually meet with strangers. If that excites you, do it. For me, an introvert, it felt like a chore, and I don't like doing chores all the time.

In contrast, there were times when I went to the other extreme. I dated no one. I personally enjoyed this more. No endless swiping and no, "So what do you do for fun?" conversations. But sometimes a reality check would pop up in my mind, *Do any single Christian men actually know I exist?* Yes, I wanted to meet someone, but I was spending my time at my dance studio—where there were no men. I was going to fitness classes with my bestie—where there were no men. And I was hanging out with my family—where there were no eligible men. Yes, I was loving all of these things, but my actions were not in alignment with what I said I wanted. I wanted a marriage partner, but I was hardly ever around anyone new.

It's important to find ways of putting yourself out there. If you want to meet someone, go places where you can meet new singles—maybe church events, maybe the gym, or maybe online dating. Again, this doesn't have to take all of your time. Do things simply because you enjoy them. And if finding a relationship is important to you, let the idea of wanting to meet new people influence some of the decisions you make. This could mean having one evening a week when you go somewhere totally different, somewhere other singles are likely to hang out. Or take just fifteen minutes before bed to interact with people on apps.

Sometimes as a single, finding 'the one' seems like the most important thing you have to focus on. This can feel overwhelming, but I don't believe it has to be an all-consuming activity. There are four buckets I believe you should spend your time in, and meeting people is just one of them. If I was single again I would spend my time in each of the four buckets—creating adventure, pursuing my gifts, growing as a person, and placing myself where I am regularly interacting with other singles.

My goal was to look back on my singleness and say that although there were some struggles and pain, this was a beautiful chapter of my life. It is cool to be standing in this blossoming relationship stage and look back with hindsight. Am I very thankful to be in a relationship? Absolutely. Relationships are beautiful things. I don't, however, feel like the triumphant escape artist. I don't feel like someone who was stranded and is finally rescued. Making intentional choices in my singleness allowed me to step into a new chapter while looking back at the last one saying, "Goodbye singleness, you were beautiful." In the ups and downs I became stronger. I didn't love every minute of singleness, but even in the tearful moments over what I was lacking came the powerful reminder of the things I already had. It was wonderful.

This is my hope for you, that no matter what part of this journey you are on, you are walking it with peace and joy, thriving, trusting in God's awesome plan for you, and no matter what trials come your way they will not knock you out. You may be single, but you are single . . . and standing.

Author's Note

"God, I am so sick of being the single, Christian, virgin girl!" I remember crying out as I was driving home one day exhausted, frustrated, and pouring my heart out to God.

What initiated this little 'conversation' with God, was that I had just been having a casual chat with a friend. We talked about life, relationships, and whatever other crazy topic we popped onto for the day. She was a newer friend, but we absolutely loved chatting with each other. It was one of those meant-to-be-friendships where right from the beginning we could finish each other's movie quotes, and we had similar thoughts, ideas, and sense of humor. It seemed as though we had covered everything in the short amount of time we had known each other. The only thing that hadn't made its way into the conversation thus far was the fact that I was a virgin. She knew I was a Christian and that my faith was a huge part of my life, but that hadn't yet translated into the *I'm saving myself for marriage so I haven't had sex yet* conversation. Until now.

In our typical random way, we were bouncing from topic to topic when my super-awesome, exciting new friend asked me how important I felt sexual intimacy was in my romantic relationships. Everything inside me froze and heated up all at once. *Nooooo! Not that question!* A million thoughts, concerns, and reasons for why I didn't want her to know, popped into my head in one big burst of tangible anxiety. Would she think I was weird? Or judge me? I loved the way that we talked openly about everything. I loved the fact that we were always on the same page. Would she feel like she had to censor herself when it came to talking about *her* relationship? Would she think that I'd judge her for living a different lifestyle?

I didn't lie. I gave her some sort of blown-off answer about how you can be intimate in lots of ways, blah, blah, blah. But then I left feeling terrible. Why did I hide a part of who I am? I felt behind and unusual, and I felt like all of this would not be a problem if only I was married like I had expected to be at this point in my life.

This is why I had that conversation with God: "God, I am *so* sick of being the single, Christian, virgin girl! I am sick of feeling unusual. I'm sick of not having sex. I'm sick of waiting to meet someone. Why do I have to wait so long for a husband? I want people to be able to talk to me. I work in places where no one else seems to be Christian and where everyone is either married or in a relationship. In my mind the correlation was clear—being the single, Christian, virgin girl was causing me to be unrelatable to people. God I am so sick of being unrelatable!"

And then I felt inside me that still small voice that I knew was God. "You'll be relatable to *them*," he said, and I knew what he meant. Immediately I could see that I share so many similarities with others. Maybe it's the people who feel odd or unusual because of their lifestyle. Maybe it's the people who are sick of being single. Maybe it's the people who are frustrated by their sexuality, whether that means they've never had sex or they are sick of trying to manage the desire. There are people out there who are feeling sick of their situations in many other ways. God was assuring me that my story would be relatable to them. The things that had been encouraging to me would benefit them too. Maybe you are one of those people. If so, this is my prayer for you.

"Lord Jesus, I pray over every person reading this book. Whatever chapter of life they are in, would you involve yourself in writing their story? As they read this prayer, would you let them know that you will create a beautiful masterpiece out of the things that just feel like splotches on the canvas of their life? Lord you see every hurt, every struggle, every place of pain and every single unmet desire.

I pray that every blessing you have planned for them will enter their life, and that they would not lack any good or perfect gift from you. Thank you for the beauty of marriage, and that so many of us desire to experience this amazing gift. I pray you would create matches that are truly miraculous. Do the unexpected, God. Do things that go beyond our imagination. Position each person reading this to follow your lead so that they can experience the fullness of your blessings. Show them how you want them to spend their time, where you want them to go, and who you want them to talk to. Guide every conversation and interaction they have so that the relationships they are meant to be in will remain, and those who are not meant for them will not. Provide them with clarity and with the strength to handle the 'no' by understanding that a 'no' is a gift because it makes space for the 'yes'. Show each person how to live this chapter of life to the fullest. Life is a gift. Each day is a gift.

You have positioned each of these people here on earth, and you care about each of their lives. Thank you for guiding them, Lord. Thank you for peace. Thank you for the ability to have faith and trust in you. Thank you for sending them the right sources of wisdom, highlighting the appropriate areas for their growth, leading their adventures, leading their dating, and leading them into your plans. I pray every person who reads this will feel encouraged and blessed in a special way. I pray for amazing times of singleness, and miraculous marriages as well. In Jesus name, Amen."

Acknowledgments

To my Mamma, Brookie, Kiersten, Evan, Jimmie, Grandma, and Grandpa. Thank you for believing I could write a book even before I did. Thank you for being my instant and unwavering supporters in this, and in all I've done. I love each of you so much. Mamma, don't worry, the first copy is yours.

To my love, Dio. To say I am thankful you walked into my life doesn't begin to describe it. Being with you has added so much beauty to both the next chapters in my life and the final chapters in my book. Thank you for your love, support, encouragement, and affirmation. I love you.

To each of my friends who encouraged me, supported me, gave me input, and became invested in this process with me—thank you. I am so grateful for your presence in my life. Also, Meghann, thank you for giving my book the gift of your artwork. It means so much to forever have your beautiful talent displayed on the cover of my writing.

And most importantly, God. This was your idea. I give this to you. All of it. The outcome, the impact, and the credit. Thank you for inspiring me, leading me, and seeing this through. This is yours.

About the Author

Brianna Rossi was born and raised in Upstate NY where she now works as a radiation therapist, teaches ballet, and loves spending time with her family. She is passionate about helping singles live thriving and joy-filled lives. She also provides singleness and dating coaching on Instagram. Connect with Brianna via:

Insta: @singleandstanding

Email: briannarossi@singleandstanding.com

Printed in the USA
CPSIA information can be obtained
at www.ICGtesting.com
LVHW020907270124
770124LV00048B/2194